✻ ι ✻ ι ✻ ι ✻ ι ✻ ι ✻ ι ✻ ι ✻ ι ✻ ι ✻ ι ✻ ι ✻ ι ✻ ι ✻

CORPORATE FINANCIAL MASTERING

Simple Methods and Strategies to Financial Analysis Mastering

✻ ι ✻ ι ✻ ι ✻ ι ✻ ι ✻ ι ✻ ι ✻ ι ✻ ι ✻ ι ✻ ι ✻ ι ✻ ι ✻

Blaine Robertson

Table of Contents

Introduction

Why do people go to doctors for checkups? It's probably for one or both reasons:

1. To stay as healthy as possible as they age; or

2. To get well from a certain sickness or medical condition.

Why do people consult with fitness professionals, e.g., trainers and coaches? It's probably for one or both reasons, too:

1. To stay as fit as possible as they age; or

2. To become fitter or to become fit again after going through something that has rendered them unfit for extended periods of time.

Now, why do people need to stay as fit and healthy as possible? It's simple; for optimal quality of life and longevity. Obviously, a sick and weak body will most likely result in lifelong suffering, which will also most likely be short. Being optimally healthy and fit maximizes the likelihood of people living a long and high quality of life.

Businesses are like people, too. They need to be optimally fit and healthy if they are to give their stakeholders optimal profitability and longevity. But instead of using blood chemistry tests, x-rays, treadmill tests, weights, and repetitions to determine a business' financial health and fitness, finance professionals use a different set of numbers, i.e., financials.

To determine a person's health and fitness, professional consultants conduct medical and fitness exams on them. To determine a business's financial health and fitness, finance professionals conduct financial analysis.

Within the pages of this book, you'll learn how to conduct financial analysis on your business or the companies whose stocks you're interested in investing in. In particular, you'll learn:

1. What are the foundations on which a business' financial health and fitness are built on;

2. What are the "raw materials," i.e., financial data, you'll need to analyze a business' financial health and fitness and more importantly, where to get them;

3. How to make sense of the financial data you have to evaluate each of the key pillars of a business' financial health and fitness; and

4. How to bring your evaluations of each key pillar together to come up with a general conclusion of a business's financial health and performance.

By the time you're done reading this book, you'll be ready to hit the ground running and start evaluating your business or other people's businesses accurately. So, turn the page now if you're ready to learn corporate financial analysis.

Chapter 1

The Four Pillars
of Financial Analysis

❀ ┃ ❀ ┃ ❀ ┃ ❀ ┃ ❀ ┃ ❀ ┃ ❀ ┃ ❀ ┃ ❀ ┃ ❀ ┃ ❀ ┃ ❀ ┃ ❀ ┃ ❀

If you remember from the introduction, the two main aspects of financial analysis are financial health and fitness. To be more consistent with the financial services industry, these two main aspects are a financial condition (health) and performance (fitness). The three main pillars upon which these two are based on are:

1. Liquidity;

2. Profitability;

3. Capital Adequacy; and

4. Asset Quality.

Liquidity

Liquidity refers to a company's ability to meet its financial obligations as they fall due. Such financial obligations include:

1. Loans with banks or financing companies;

2. Credit purchases from suppliers;

3. Salaries of employees; and

4. Utility bills.

The reason why liquidity is at the top of our financial analysis food chain is simple; without cash, businesses will grind to a halt. Never mind if a business is very profitable and has adequate capital. If it doesn't have enough cash, its suppliers, creditors, and employees will stop supplying them with needed resources to continue operating.

Now, you may be wondering is it possible to be profitable and have enough capital and yet, be illiquid, i.e., not have enough money to meet financial obligations? Yes, it is.

To understand how this is so, you'll need to know the two main ways financial transactions are recorded under accounting rules; cash basis and accrual basis.

Under the cash basis, income is recorded only when cash is received. Also, expenses are recorded only when cash is disbursed.

Under the accrual basis, income is recorded as soon a business has sold products or rendered services, not when it receives cash payments for them. Expenses are recorded when they're incurred, i.e., the business has already received products or services, not when they've paid for them already.

Most, if not all, businesses, especially corporations, use the accrual basis for recording financial transactions. Businesses that sell products or provide services mostly on credit have higher liquidity risks compared to those that sell mostly in cash. Why?

Let's compare two businesses, Company A and Company B. Both companies have:

1. Annual sales of $100,000;

2. Total annual expenses of $50,000;

3. Annual debt payments (not expenses) of $30,000;

4. Annual net income of $50,000; and

5. Cash balance of $10,000.

However, 50% of Company A's sales, i.e., $50,000, were on credit and payable in one year. This means Company A only receives $50,000 in cash annually, which is less than its total annual financial obligations (operating expenses + debt payments). Even using its cash reserves of $10,000, it will only have $60,000, which is still less than its annual financial obligation of $80,000.

This means Company A isn't able to meet all of its annual financial obligations amounting to $80,000, and as such, it's illiquid. Yes, it's very profitable with a $50,000 annual net income, but because 50% of its sales are on credit, little cash is coming in compared to the cash it has to payout.

Compare it to Company B, whose credit sales only comprise 20% of total annual. Thus, its annual cash sales are $80,000, which is already equal to its annual financial obligations of $ 80,000. Its annual cash sales alone already make it a liquid company, even without taking into consideration the $10,000 in cash reserves.

Now, let's look at the flip side. Let's say both Companies A and B have:

1. Annual sales of $100,000;

2. Total annual expenses (all paid in cash) of $105,000;

3. Annual debt payments (not expenses) of $10,000;

4. Annual net loss of $10,000: and

5. Cash balance of $50,000.

This time, Company A's credit sales account for 70% of annual sales or $70,000. This gives it annual cash receipts totaling $70,000. But its annual financial obligations of $115,000 (expenses + debt payments) is still greater than its annual cash receipts. However, adding its cash balance of $50,000 makes it able to pay all of its $115,000 financial obligations for the year, with $5,000 extra:

Total Annual Expenses (all paid in cash) = $110,000

Annual Debt Obligations = $5,000

Total Annual Financial Obligations = $115,000

Annual Cash Receipts = $70,000

Cash Balance = $50,000

Total Cash Available for Obligations = $120,000

Now, this is a simple illustration, but it's easy enough to understand to drive home the importance of liquidity.

Profitability

The primary goal of putting up a business is to make money, i.e., earn profits. Even non-profit organizations need to figure out how to make profits through donations and pledges because if they spend more than what they earn, they'll eventually become illiquid and cease operations.

Liquidity is more concerned about current financial health, while profitability is more concerned about sustaining financial health. Given the example of how a losing business can still be liquid despite losing money, such liquidity can't be sustained without continuous profits.

Relying on continuous capital infusions to sustain liquidity and financial health is a stupid idea. If the primary goal of putting up a business is to make money, why would investors continue putting in money in a business that continuously loses it? Might as well donate the money to the charity where it'll make a difference.

Sustained profitability is key to financial longevity. Thus, this should be the primary metric by which you measure a company's financial fitness or performance.

Operational Efficiency

How a company operates or uses its resources is key to its success and failures. The more a company's ability to use its resources efficiently, the lower its costs become, the higher its revenues climb, and the greater its net income becomes. The less efficient it becomes at doing so, the higher its expenses can be, and the lower its revenues may become.

When it comes to operating efficiency, there are two main areas that you'll need to focus on as an analyst: inventory movement and collection of receivables. Why?

Inventory movement refers to how fast a company is able to move inventory out of its custody into the possession of customers. In short, it's about how fast a company sells its inventories.

Why is that important? The longer inventories stay in a company's possession, the less cash is available for the company to use for its operations. In a sense, it can affect a company's liquidity.

Slow-moving inventories also mean fewer sales, which leads to reduced sales revenues. Hence, it can also impact profitability.

The other important aspect of operating efficiency is the collection of receivables, i.e., how fast a company's ability to collect payments on its credit sales to customers. You see, credit sales can help boost revenues, but if not managed wisely, it can result in overdue accounts that can impact liquidity, too. And a lot of credit sales turn sour; it's going to impact profitability as well.

Operating efficiency is the long-term key to long-term liquidity and profitability. That's why people should never underestimate it.

Solvency

The company funds its assets in two ways: owners' money (capital) and debt (liabilities). While a company can be funded entirely with capital from owners, it can't be funded entirely with debt. No financial institution will be crazy enough to lend to businesses wherein the owners didn't put in their own money in them.

That being said, capital is the ultimate barometer of financial health and a business' longevity. Companies that file for bankruptcy are those whose capital balances are already negative, i.e., the value of their debts or financial obligations is greater than the value of their assets. In short, they no longer have enough assets to satisfy their financial obligations with their creditors.

You see, when the value of a company's assets is higher than its debts, it can still pay for them by selling assets. It can use the cash proceeds to pay for its debts.

But when the value of the debts is greater than the value of the assets, i.e., negative capitalization, selling all of its assets will not be enough for a company to settle its debts. Hence, bankruptcy.

The primary factors that affect a company's capital adequacy are, you guessed it:

1. Profitability;

2. Liquidity; and

3. Operational Efficiency.

When a company suffers net losses, these are charged against its capital. If a company loses an average of $10,000 annually and its current capital is at $50,000, you can expect the company to go bankrupt after 5 years.

The larger the net losses, the faster capital is depleted, and the higher the risks for bankruptcy.

When a company becomes illiquid, it's forced to borrow money to cover for its shortfall. If perennially short on cash and borrowing more money, it will come to a point when its debts will exceed the value of its assets. Thus, illiquidity can also lead to bankruptcy.

Finally, asset quality impacts both a company's ability to make money (profitability) and its liquidity. Poor asset quality heightens a company's risks for net losses and illiquidity, which both increase bankruptcy risks.

Chapter 2

The Raw Materials Needed
for Financial Analysis

You can't conduct even a simple financial analysis just by looking at a company's stock price, the news, or how many people patronize it. Why?

Look no further than the company Enron, which is one of the biggest, if not the biggest, cases of corporate failure in history. By all external accounts, Enron appears to be a very strong and healthy company based on asset size and revenues alone. But of course, we know how it all turned out, right?

Or how about the most recent corporate failure, though at a much smaller scale, involving Forever 21? It filed for bankruptcy in September 2019. On the surface, it looks like a thriving business, but financial analysts weren't really surprised because they knew, based on regular financial evaluations of the company, that it was already on the road to perdition months or years prior.

To conduct simple yet accurate financial evaluations of a company's financial health and fitness, you'll need the right kinds of raw materials. And these raw materials are financial information, which you can get from:

1. Financial Statements;

2. Market Data on Financial Securities; and

3. Economic Data.

Financial Statements

Financial statements refer to financial records that reflect a company's financial condition and performance. There are three important kinds of financial statements:

1. The Statement of Condition or Balance Sheet;

2. The Statement of Income and Expenses or Income Statement; and

3. Statement of Cash Flows.

Balance Sheet

As the name suggests, the Balance Sheet reflects the current balances of a company's asset, liability, and capital accounts as of a specific date, usually the end of a year, quarter, or month. The balance sheet reflects:

1. The dollar values of the assets a company owns;

2. How much a company owes to other people or companies; and

3. The dollar value of owners' capital contributions, including income that's reinvested into the business.

The Income Statement

This type of financial statement tells you how much money the company made or lost for a specific period of time, e.g., annual, quarterly, or monthly. For accounting and taxation purposes, annual income statements are used. But of course, there's nothing that'll keep you from analyzing a company's monthly or quarterly results of operations, which can be very useful as you'll see later on.

The Cash Flow Statement

Remember earlier during our discussion on liquidity, how being profitable doesn't necessarily mean liquidity and vice versa? Well, the purpose of the cash flow statement is to show how much money a company received and paid for a specific period of time. More importantly, it gives a detailed breakdown of where money was paid out and from where the company received it.

The cash flow statement is very important for evaluating a company's liquidity because it presents both the net cash received or paid for the time period and its exact details, i.e., where the money came from and went to. Such details can help you determine a company's liquidity risk moving forward.

Market Data on Financial Securities

What do these types of information, e.g., stock market prices, bond prices, and ratios have to do with financial analysis of an individual company? Well, they help give you context regarding the results of your analysis.

For example, your financial analysis of a company may have shown it registers an average annual return on investment of 10%, which means it's profitable as any figure above 0% means the company earned more than what it spent. But if you're interested in investing in that company, you'll need to know if that company will give you the best return or if there are other more profitable investment opportunities.

Market data such as average annual return on stock market investments and price-earnings ratios of other similar companies or of the whole industry give you a benchmark by which to evaluate. If the average annual return on blue-chip stocks on the New York Stock Exchange is 13%, a 10% return on investment isn't enough to make a much smaller company worthy of your investment. Why?

First, you have the option of putting your money in blue-chip stocks, which have a higher average annual return. Second, blue-chip stocks in major exchanges like the NYSE and NASDAQ provide very high liquidity, i.e., you can easily convert your investment back into cash if you need money. The same can't be said with investments in companies that aren't listed in any major stock exchange.

In terms of financial ratios, which we'll talk about later, market data on (competitors or the industry) also gives you an objective benchmark for evaluation. Take, for example, the price-to-earnings (P/E) ratio, which indicates how high or cheap the price of a share of stock is. A higher P/E ratio indicates that a share of stock is expensive, while a lower one means it's cheaper. So, between two stocks with P/E ratios of 10 times and 20 times, the one with the P/E ratio of 10 times is the bargain, i.e., a better buy. We'll get into the P/E ratio later in Chapter 7 on evaluating value.

You may think that the value of a company's shares is already cheap based on your subjective criteria, but unless you compare it to that of similar companies and/or the industry's, you run the risk of actually buying overpriced stock.

Economic Data

When the general economy's doing poorly, the chances are that companies, in general, won't do well either. That's why you'll also need to consider economic data for financial analysis in some cases.

Take, for example, interest rates. Many companies use debt to finance their operations and expansion plans. When interest rates go up, the borrowing costs of these companies. Higher interest rates mean larger interest payments, higher expenses, and smaller income or greater losses.

Another important economic data to consider is GDP or gross national product, which is the primary barometer for saying whether or not a country's economy is growing.

If GDP is positive and is expected to continue staying positive, it means the general economy is expected to continue growing in the foreseeable future. Obviously, this is good for any business. If negative, i.e., a recession or economic contraction, then businesses are at high risk for reduced revenues and income, too.

Chapter 3

Important Financial
Analysis Principles

When you look at numbers on a company's financial statements, those numbers won't mean much to you. Why?

So, what if the company's cash balance is $1 million? What does it tell you other than it has a million dollars at the end of a certain date? What's the significance of registering a net income of $100 thousand for the last fiscal year other than it made $100 thousand?

They don't tell you anything meaningful about the company unless you relate them to other figures. There are two ways you can perform financial analysis by comparing different financial statement numbers: horizontal analysis and vertical analysis.

Vertical Analysis

This refers to the practice of relating a specific account balance in a company's financial statement with another account balance for the same time period. A good example is comparing the end-of-year total current assets to the end-of-year total current liabilities.

If you may recall, current assets are assets that a company can easily convert into cash with the next 12 months. Current liabilities, on the other hand, are liabilities that a company needs to pay within the next 12 months.

A year-end total current assets balance of $10 million dollars looks very impressive, eh? Not when the company has a year-end total current liabilities balance of $15 million. With current assets less than current liabilities, the risk of not being able to meet financial obligations, i.e., pay liabilities when they fall due, is high.

On the other hand, a year-end total current assets balance of only $100 thousand dollars may sound unimpressive at face value. But if the company's year-end total current liabilities balance is only $10,000, it speaks of the company's very high liquidity, having more than enough cash and near-cash assets to pay for liabilities due within the next 12 months.

Another very good example of the importance of vertical analysis relates to evaluating a company's profitability. A $10 million-dollar net income for the year looks very impressive at first glance. But if you compare it to the total year-end equity or capital balance of $300 million, that net income represents a measly 3.33% return on investment.

Financial ratios are computed using vertical analysis. Remember the price-to-earnings (P/E) ratio example I gave earlier? This ratio is computed by dividing a stock's current price over its earnings-per-share (EPS) ratio. The EPS is computed by dividing total net income for the previous year over the total outstanding shares as of the end of that year. The EPS requires vertical analysis of a company's financial accounts (number of shares outstanding and net income) while the P/E ratio involves vertical analysis of financial statement data (EPS) and market data (current stock price).

Horizontal Analysis

Horizontal analysis is another term used for time-series analysis. If vertical analysis aims to make sense of financial statement and market information by relating different accounts for the same time period or cut-off date, the horizontal analysis aims to show changes in said accounts and/or financial ratios derived through vertical analysis.

Horizontal or time series analysis tells you whether the company is progressing, regressing, or has plateaued in terms of specific areas or metrics. This is very important in terms of risk management because, through horizontal analysis, management can spot problems and address them before it's too late.

Again, let's take a look at net income as an example. If company A's net income for the previous fiscal year is $10 million, it may seem good or even impressive at first glance, right? But what if the net income the year before that and two years before that were $15 million and $20 million respectively? Your evaluation would change from very satisfactory to alarming because it's the second straight year of significant decline.

By spotting the fast decline in the company's profitability, specifically net income, management can focus on identifying which components of profitability have become problematic. Is it declining revenues, increasing operating expenses, or both?

Industry and Inter-Securities Analysis

If you want a complete financial analysis of a company's true financial condition and performance, consider comparing its financial metrics with those of its competitors. Why?

Peer comparisons can give a company's stakeholders ideas of what's possible in terms of improvement and whether the company's the best available investment. For example, if you want to invest in shares of stock of an electronics company, one of the things you'd like to check is the probability of it giving you the best possible returns. And you can only do that by comparing annual rates of return and profitability of that electronics company to those of its competitors or industry peers.

That company's shares of stock may have an average annual return of 10%, which is already good in most cases. But what if some of its peers have an average annual return of 15%? While 10% is already good, you would've missed out on opportunities to earn potentially higher returns or at least diversify your investments such that you get a higher average return on investment than 10%.

Aside from peer comparisons, it will also be much better to conduct a financial analysis of a company in light of industry averages and developments. This is particularly important in terms of projected sales and income growth.

You can easily tell whether a company's management team's projected sales and income growth for the next five years is reasonable or not by comparing it with the average growth of its industry. Do you think a projected average annual sales growth rate of 50% is reasonable when the industry average is only 10%, and the projected 5-year growth rate is only 12% per year?

Inter-securities analysis means comparing metrics, particularly returns on investments, with other financial assets or securities. For example, a friend is offering you an opportunity to partner with him in a new restaurant business, which he conservatively projects to give an average annual return on investment of 10%.

Before taking on the offer, why not check out returns on investment of other financial assets such as stocks of publicly-listed companies, which have much lower financial and liquidity risks. By virtue of being listed in major stock exchanges, such companies have much lower financial risks, and their stocks offer high liquidity. Not only will you have lower risks for investment losses, but you can also easily convert your investments in stocks of publicly-listed companies to cash, compared to an actual brick-and-mortar business.

If the conservative estimated ROI on the restaurant business is 50%, then it might be worth the risk. But if it's just a few percentage points higher than that of publicly-traded stocks, you'd be better off with the latter.

Compounding and Discounting

Compounding refers to the practice of computing for a future value given the following variables:

1. Beginning amount (Principal or Present Value);

2. Interest, growth, or compounding rate;

3. Time (in years); and

4. Compounding frequency, e.g., monthly, quarterly, or annually;

Compounding is an important principle to use when making simple financial forecasts for a company and estimating risks. For example, one can reasonably estimate a company's expenses in the next one, two, and three years using inflation as growth or compounding rate.

The formula for compounding, i.e., computing for future value is:

Future Value = Present Value X [1 + {Annual Rate ÷ Compounding Frequency}]Frequency X Years

Unless otherwise stated, compounding frequency is annual, i.e., once a year only.

For example, if current operating expenses are $50,000, and the average inflation rate for the last 10 years is 1%, then estimated operating expenses two years from now would be:

Future Value = $50,000 X [1 + {0.01 ÷ 1}]1 X 2 Years

Future Value = $50,000 X [1.01]2 Years

Future Value = $50,000 X [1.0201]

Future Value = $51,005.00

Discounting, on the other hand, is the reverse-engineering equivalent of compounding, i.e., computing for the principal amount or present value, given an expected maturity or future value. It involves the same variables, except that instead of the principal amount, the future value or maturity value is used.

This is very useful for making decisions like whether a certain investment is worth the price. Companies' financial analysts compute for the present value of an investment and compare it to the price at which it's being offered or its current cost. If the price or cost is lower than the discounted or present value, it's a go. Otherwise, it's a no.

The formula for discounting is derived from the one of compounding, using basic algebra, i.e.:

Present Value = Future Value ÷ [1 + {Annual Rate ÷ Compounding Frequency}]Frequency X Years

If the maturity value of a non-coupon paying bond is $10,000 after 10 years and its current yield is 2%, then its value today is:

Present Value = $10,000 ÷ [1 + {.02 ÷ 1}]1 X 10

Present Value = $10,000 ÷ [1 .02]10

Present Value = $10,000 ÷ [1 .02]10

Present Value = $10,000 ÷ 1.2190

Present Value = $8,203.48

The selling price of this particular bond with an annual yield of 2.00% that will mature at $10,000 in 10 years is $8,203.48

Using the same formula, you can also get a reasonable estimate of the average annual growth or decline of a specific account in a company's financial statements. Using basic algebra again, the formula for estimating growth rate based on the original compounding formula is:

Annual Rate = [{Future Value ÷ Present Value}1÷(frequency X years) – 1] X Compounding Frequency

Using our earlier example of the non-coupon paying bond due in ten years:

Annual Rate = [{$10,000 ÷ $8,203.48}1÷(1 X 10) – 1] X 1

Annual Rate = [{1.2190}1÷(10) – 1] X 1

Annual Rate = [{1.2190}0.10 – 1] X 1

Annual Rate = [1.02 – 1] X 1

Annual Rate = 0.02 X 1

Annual Rate = 0.02 or 2.00%

Another specific example of using the compounding principle to estimate the average annual growth rate is operating expenses. Let's say that a company's operating expenses for the last five years were the following:

2018 2017 2016 2015 2014

$15,000.00 $14,100.00 $13,600.00 $13,700.00 $12,900.00

The present amount or value, in this case, is $12,900, which is the operating expenses for 2014. The future or ending value is $15,000, which is the operating expenses for 2018. Compounding frequency is annual (unless otherwise stated), and the number of years is four (2014 is the base, hence only 4 years of compounding).

Using the formula, you can estimate the average annual growth rate in operating expenses:

Average Annual Growth Rate = [{$15,000 ÷ $12,900}1÷(1 X 4) – 1] X 1

Average Annual Growth Rate = [{1.1628}1÷(4) – 1] X 1

Average Annual Growth Rate = [{1.1628}0.25 – 1] X 1

Average Annual Growth Rate = [1.0384 – 1] X 1

Average Annual Growth Rate = 0.0384 X 1

Average Annual Growth Rate = 0.0384 or 3.84%

To estimate operating expenses the year after, use the annual rate to compound 2018's operating expenses:

Future Value = Present Value X [1 + {Annual Rate ÷ Compounding Frequency}]Frequency X Years

Estimated 2019 Operating Expenses = $15,000 X [1 + {0.0384 ÷ 1}]1 X 1 Year

Estimated 2019 Operating Expenses = $15,000 X [1.0384]1 Year

Estimated 2019 Operating Expenses = $15,000 X [1.0384]

Estimated 2019 Operating Expenses = $15,576.38

Volatility

Volatility refers to the tendency for something, such as a stock price, to veer away from its average. It helps you estimate risks in a more objective form, i.e., through numbers.

For example, if the average annual return on the stock market is 10%, it doesn't mean that your stock investments will always grow by 10% every year. There's a likelihood that the returns on stocks may be higher than 10% or less than 10%. In other words, chances are very high that future returns on such investments will deviate from the average based on past performance. That's volatility.

The simplest way to estimate volatility is through standard deviation. This gives you an idea of more or less how much returns on your investments or growth rates in the balance sheet and income statement assets will fall short or exceed the average. In short, the standard deviation can help you establish a reasonable band of figures within which expected or future results will most likely lie.

For example, if the average annual growth rate of a company's sales for the last 10 years has been 5%, and the standard deviation is 2%, it means that one can reasonably expect sales to grow between a minimum of 3% (5% - 2%) and a maximum of 7% (5% + 2%).

So, if you want to be conservative when estimating growth forecasts, you can use the minimum figure, i.e., average growth rate, less standard deviation.

When it comes to choosing investments, the standard deviation can give you an idea of the least amount of return a company may reasonably get from that specific investment. For example, if the shares of Stock A appreciates at an average annual rate of 10% with a standard deviation of 15%, then at best, you may get an annual return of 25% (10% + 15%) or at worst, a 5% loss (10% - 15%).

This is how you can compare investment apples and oranges properly. For example, will you choose Investment A with an average annual rate of return of 10% or Investment B with only 8%? At first glance, Investment A appears to be the wiser choice. But what if Investment A's standard deviation is 4% and Investment B's is only 1%? Let's take a look:

1. Investment A's expected range of returns is between 6% (10% - 4%) and 14% (10% + 4%); and

2. Investment B's expected range of returns is between 7% (8% - 1%) and 9% (8% + 1%).

Based on these numbers, Investment B has a higher minimum investment return at 7%, while Investment A has a higher maximum expected return on investments. For a conservative investor, the wise option is Investment B, with a higher minimum return. For a more aggressive or risk-taking investor, the wise choice is Investment A with a higher maximum expected rate of return.

Here's another example: Investment A with average annual returns of 5% and a standard deviation of 6% and Investment B with average returns of 3% and a standard deviation of 1%.

The range of minimum and maximum returns for Investment A are -1% (5% - 6%) and 11% (5% + 6%), respectively. On the other hand, the range of minimum and maximum returns for Investment B are 2% (3% - 1%) and 4% (3% + 1%), respectively.

For conservative investors, Investment B is a clear choice, with a minimum expected return of 2% vs. Investment B's potential investment loss of 1%. On the other hand, aggressive investors will most likely choose Investment A, with a higher maximum expected return of 11% vs. Investment B's maximum of only 4%.

Chapter 4

Liquidity

❊ ❊ ❊ ❊ ❊ ❊ ❊ ❊ ❊ ❊ ❊ ❊ ❊ ❊

As mentioned earlier, liquidity refers to a company's ability to meet its financial obligations when they're due. In short, liquidity refers to how much cash or near-cash balances a company has for paying its bills and debts.

When making conclusions about a company's liquidity, you can say any of the following:

1. The company's liquidity risk, i.e., the risk of not being able to meet its financial obligations, is high, low, or moderate; and

2. The company is liquid, not very liquid, very liquid, or illiquid (unable to meet its financial obligations).

What'll be your basis for making liquidity conclusions about a company? You can use the following liquidity ratios:

1. Current Ratio;

2. Quick Ratio;

3. Sales-to-Receivables Ratio;

4. Days' Receivables Ratio; and

5. Cash Turnover Ratio.

Let's take a look at each of them in more detail.

Current Ratio

This ratio is computed by dividing total current assets over total current liabilities. Current assets are those that are either in cash form or near-cash form (can be converted into cash within the next 12 months). These include:

1. Cash balances (cash on hand, cash in banks);

2. Accounts receivables (credit sales, etc.);

3. Marketable securities (investments in publicly-traded securities like stocks and bonds); and

4. Inventories.

On the other hand, current liabilities refer to financial obligations that are due within the next 12 months. These include:

1. Utility bills;

2. Salaries payable;

3. Supplies and inventory purchased on credit;

4. Loans and mortgages due to in the next 12 months; and

5. Other financial obligations due within the next 12 months, e.g., court-imposed penalties and charges.

The current ratio gives you an idea of a company's ability to pay current financial obligations. If current assets equal current liabilities, the current ratio will be 1.

If the company has more current assets than current liabilities, its current ratio will be greater than 1, which means it has more than enough to meet its current obligations. The higher the current ratio is, the more liquid a company is.

However, if the company's current assets are less than its current liabilities, its current ratio will be less than 1. It means that the company is illiquid, or isn't able to fulfill its current financial obligations as of the financial statements' date.

While there isn't any official benchmark for current ratios, many financial analysts believe that a current ratio of 2.0 is ideal. And while a higher current ratio is more desirable than a lower one, a very high current ratio shouldn't be something to celebrate either. Why?

Companies always strive to maintain the right balance of liquidity and profitability. If a company has too much cash or near cash assets, its profitability suffers because these assets don't make much money. So, very high liquidity limits a company's profitability.

On the other hand, focusing too much on profitability can result in significantly low cash or near-cash balance vis-a-vis current liabilities. Especially if the bulk of a company's sales is in the form of credit, there's a great risk that the company may become illiquid, too.

Again, there's no magic number for current ratios, but the consensus among most financial analysts and CFOs is a current ratio of two is the ideal one.

Quick Ratio, i.e., the Acid-Test Ratio

This is a stricter version of the current ratio, which excludes inventories from current assets. Why?

Inventories, though convertible to cash within the year, isn't a near-cash asset. It will take at least several weeks or months to sell all of a company's inventories, which isn't a quick liquidation.

On the other hand, cash (on hand and from banks) is already cash and accounts receivables, and marketable securities can be easily converted into cash within days. Other than the immediate collection of accounts receivables, they can be sold or discounted in exchange for cash, while marketable securities like stocks can be easily sold in major exchanges.

As with the current ratio, there's no official benchmark or standard, but the ideal consensus is a minimum of 1.0.

Sales-to-Receivables Turnover Ratio

This ratio tells how fast a company is able to collect on its credit sales in terms of the number of cycles per year. The higher the number, the more cycles or turnovers happen, which implies a shorter collection period. The lower the number, the fewer cycles or turnovers happen during a year, which means longer or extended collection period.

This is an important liquidity metric in that it gives an idea of how inventories, particularly those sold under credit, are converted into cash. The faster the turnover, the faster the company receives cash from credit sales, which can contribute to lower liquidity risk. The slower the turnover, the longer it takes for a company to receive cash from its credit sales, which may contribute to higher liquidity risk.

Sales-to-Receivables Turnover ratio is computed by dividing net sales by average accounts receivables.

Days Receivables

This measure tells you the average number of days a company needs to collect on its receivables. Obviously, the lower the number, the faster it collects on credit sales, which contributes to lower liquidity risk. A higher number means a longer collection period for receivables, which can contribute to higher liquidity risk.

Days Receivables is computed by dividing 365 days by the sales-to-receivables turnover ratio.

Cash Turnover Ratio

This ratio gives you an idea of a company's ability to finance its current operations, how well it uses working capital, and how much protection leeway its creditors enjoy. You can compute for a company's cash turnover ratio by dividing annual net sales over its average net working capital for the year. Net working capital is the difference between current assets and current liabilities.

Most analysts agree that the ideal ratio is between five and six times the average net working capital. The higher the ratio, the more vulnerable a company is to its creditors because it signals that a big chunk of its sales is funded by borrowed money. On the other hand, a very low ratio isn't good, too, because it means it has too much working capital, i.e., a company's using its working capital inefficiently.

Example: Apple, Inc.

To help you grasp the concept of liquidity better, let's compute for Apple, Inc.'s liquidity ratios, and based on that, make conclusions about how liquid the company is. For that, let's use the company's submitted balance sheets and income statements from fiscal years ending in 2015 to 2019.

Apple Inc.

CONSOLIDATED BALANCE SHEETS

For Fiscal Years Ending September 30

In Millions, Except for Fiscal Year-End Stock Prices in Actual Amounts

	2019	2018	2017	2016	2015
ASSETS:					
Current assets:					
Cash and cash equivalents	$ 48,844.00	$ 25,913.00	$ 20,289.00	$ 20,484.00	$ 21,120.00
Marketable securities	$ 51,713.00	$ 40,388.00	$ 53,892.00	$ 46,671.00	$ 20,481.00
Accounts receivable, net	$ 22,926.00	$ 23,186.00	$ 17,874.00	$ 15,754.00	$ 16,849.00
Inventories	$ 4,106.00	$ 3,956.00	$ 4,855.00	$ 2,132.00	$ 2,349.00
Vendor non-trade receivables	$ 22,878.00	$ 25,809.00	$ 17,799.00	$ 13,545.00	$ 13,494.00
Other current assets	$ 12,352.00	$ 12,087.00	$ 13,936.00	$ 8,283.00	$ 15,085.00
Total current assets	$ 162,819.00	$ 131,339.00	$ 128,645.00	$106,869.00	$ 89,378.00
Non-current assets:					
Marketable securities	$ 105,341.00	$ 170,799.00	$ 194,714.00	$170,430.00	$ 164,065.00
Property, plant and equipment, net	$ 37,378.00	$ 41,304.00	$ 33,783.00	$ 27,010.00	$ 22,471.00

Other non-current assets	$ 32,978.00	$ 22,283.00	$ 18,177.00	$ 17,377.00	$ 14,431.00
Total non-current assets	$ 175,697.00	$ 234,386.00	$ 246,674.00	$ 214,817.00	$ 200,967.00
Total assets	**$ 338,516.00**	**$ 365,725.00**	**$ 375,319.00**	**$321,686.0**	**$290,345.00**

LIABILITIES AND SHAREHOLDERS' EQUITY:

Current liabilities:

Accounts payable	$ 46,236.00	$ 55,888.00	$ 44,242.00	$ 37,294.00	$ 35,490.00
Other current liabilities	$ 37,720.00	$ 32,687.00	$ 30,551.00	$ 22,027.00	$ 25,181.00
Deferred revenue	$ 5,522.00	$ 7,543.00	$ 7,548.00	$ 8,080.00	$ 8,940.00
Commercial paper	$ 5,980.00	$ 11,964.00	$ 11,977.00	$ 8,105.00	$ 8,499.00
Term debt	$ 10,260.00	$ 8,784.00	$ 6,496.00	$ 3,500.00	$ 2,500.00
Total current liabilities	**$ 105,718.00**	**$116,866.00**	**$ 100,814.00**	**$79,006.00**	**$80,610.00**

Non-current liabilities:

Deferred revenue		$ 2,797.00	$ 2,836.00	$ 2,930.00	$ 3,624.00
Term debt	$ 91,807.00	$ 93,735.00	$ 97,207.00	$ 75,427.00	$ 53,329.00
Other non-current liabilities	$ 50,503.00	$ 45,180.00	$ 40,415.00	$ 36,074.00	$ 33,427.00
Total non-current liabilities	*$ 142,310.00*	*$ 141,712.00*	*$ 140,458.00*	*$114,431.0*	*$ 90,380.00*
Total liabilities	**$ 248,028.00**	**$ 258,578.00**	**$ 241,272.00**	**$193,437.0**	**$ 170,990.00**

Commitments and contingencies

Shareholders' equity:

Common stock and additional paid-in capital, $0.00001 par value: 12,600,000 shares authorized; 4,754,986 and 5,126,201 shares issued and outstanding, respectively	$ 45,174.00	$ 40,201.00	$ 35,867.00	$ 31,251.00	$ 27,416.00
Retained earnings	$ 45,898.00	$ 70,400.00	$ 98,330.00	$ 96,364.00	$ 92,284.00
Accumulated other comprehensive income/(loss)	$ (584.00)	$ (3,454.00)	$ (150.00)	$ 634.00	$ (345.00)

Total shareholders' equity	*$ 90,488.00*	*$ 107,147.00*	*$ 134,047.00*	*$128,249.0*	*$ 119,355.00*
Total liabilities and shareholders' equity	$ 338,516.00	$ 365,725.00	$ 375,319.00	$321,686.0	$ 290,345.00
Net Working Capital	$ 57,101.00	$ 14,473.00	$ 27,831.00	$27,863.00	$ 8,768.00
Fiscal Year-End Stock Prices	$ 248.02	$ 214.87	$ 163.49	$ 107.91	$ 111.19

Apple, Inc.
CONSOLIDATED STATEMENTS OF OPERATIONS
Fiscal Years Ending in September 30
In millions, Except Number of Shares Which are Reflected in Thousands and Per Share Amounts

	2019	2018	2017	2016	2015
	$ 2,019	$ 2,018	$ 2,017	$ 2,016	$ 2,015
Net sales:					
Products	$ 213,883	$ 225,847	$ 196,534		
Services	$ 46,291	$ 39,748	$ 32,700		
Total net sales	$ 260,174	$ 265,595	$ 229,234	$ 215,639	$ 233,715
*Theoretical Credit Sales	$ 110,000	$ 150,000	$ 130,000	$ 90,000	$ 120,000
Cost of sales:					
Total cost of sales	*$ 161,782*	*$ 163,756*	*$ 141,048*	*$ 131,376*	*$ 140,089*
Gross margin	$ 98,392	$ 101,839	$ 88,186	$ 84,263	$ 93,626
Operating expenses:					
Research and development	$ 16,217	$ 14,236	$ 11,581	$ 10,045	$ 8,067
Selling, general and administrative	$ 18,245	$ 16,705	$ 15,261	$ 14,194	$ 14,329
Total operating expenses	*$ 34,462*	*$ 30,941*	*$ 26,842*	*$ 24,239*	*$ 22,396*

Operating income	**$ 63,930**	**$ 70,898**	**$ 61,344**	**$ 60,024**	**$ 71,230**
Other income/(expense), net	$ 1,807	$ 2,005	$ 2,745	$ 1,348	$ 1,285
Income before provision for income taxes	**$ 65,737**	**$ 72,903**	**$ 64,089**	**$ 61,372**	**$ 72,515**
Provision for income taxes	$ 10,481	$ 13,372	$ 15,738	$ 15,685	$ 19,121
Net income	**$55,256**	**$ 59,531**	**$48,351**	**$45,687**	**$53,394**
Earnings per share:					
Basic	$ 12	$ 12	$ 9	$ 8	$ 9
Shares used in computing earnings per share:					
Basic	$ 4,617,834	$4,955,377	$5,217,242	$5,470,820	$5,753,421

Here are the liquidity ratios for the fiscal years ending in September 30 from 2016 to 2019:

Liquidity Ratios	**2019**	**2018**	**2017**	**2016**	**2015**
Current Ratio (Current Assets/Current Liabilities)	1.54	1.12	1.28	1.35	1.11
Quick Ratio Quick Assets (cash, marketable securities, and receivables)/Current Liabilities	1.17	0.77	0.91	1.05	0.73
Sales-to-Receivables (Turnover) Ratio (Net Sales/Accounts Receivable)	11.35	11.45	12.82	13.69	13.87
Days' Receivables (365/Sales to receivables ratio)	32.16	31.86	28.46	26.67	26.31
Cash Turnover Ratio (Net Sales/Net Working Capital)	4.56	18.35	8.24	7.74	26.66

What can you say about its current and quick ratios? Given that the ideal current and quick ratios are 2.0 and 1.0, respectively, we can say that:

1. As of 2019, Apple, Inc. is liquid, i.e., it has more than enough current and quick assets to meet its financial obligations for the next 12 months; and

2. After 2 years of decline in liquidity, it has improved in the fiscal year 2019. And while its current ratio is less than the ideal minimum of 2.0, it still has more than enough current assets to cover current liabilities, and its quick assets ratio is above the minimum 1.0.

Let's take a look at the sales-to-receivables turnover ratio and days receivables, which give us an idea of how fast – or slow – Apple, Inc., collects on its credit sales. From the ratios computed, we can conclude that Apple's ability to collect on receivables has slowed down in the last three to four years, with sales-to-receivables ratio and days receivables at five-year lows and highs, respectively. However, the slow down isn't significant because it was only a matter of days.

Another way to make sense of the day's receivables ratio is by comparing it to the company's credit terms, i.e., how many days it gives customers to pay for credit sales. In theory, what if Apple gives all of its credit customers up to 30 days to pay for their credit purchases? The day's receivables figure of 32.16 days for the fiscal year 2019 is over two days longer than the credit terms given to customers. Therefore, this means Apple is having problems enforcing its collection policies.

But what if the company gives customers up to 60 days to pay for their credit purchases? The 32.16 days receivables number is much lower than the company's credit terms, which means that the company is very efficient in collecting from its customers. Also, it may indicate that its 60-days credit terms are too long and that they can shorten it to, say, 45 days to improve liquidity.

Finally, let's look at the cash turnover ratios for the fiscal years ending September 2016 to 2019. Based on the numbers, we can say that Apple's working capital efficiency has dropped substantially, which requires a deeper analysis. After three straight years of increasing efficiency, peaking at 18.35 times net working capital during the fiscal year 2018, it dropped precipitously to only 4.56 for the fiscal year ending September 2019.

What could be the reason for this? It may be one of three things:

1. A substantial drop in net sales;

2. A substantial increase in net working capital; or

3. Both.

When you look at the income statement, net sales is just slightly lower than in 2018, which registered the highest net sales in the last five years. So clearly, it wasn't a case of a major drop in sales.

But looking at the balance sheet, you can see that the net working capital jumped to $57 billion, which was its highest level in the last five years. This is almost 3 times higher than the previous fiscal year's net working capital level of only $14 billion.

If you dig even deeper why the net working capital balance puffed up, you'll see it was because of the substantial increase in cash and marketable securities during the fiscal year 2019. From balances of $25.9 and $40.4 billion at the end of the fiscal year 2018 for cash and marketable securities, respectively, both jumped in 2019. Cash ended the fiscal year 2019 with a balance of $48.8 billion, while marketable securities ended up with $51.7 billion.

Putting It Together: Liquidity

To come up with a general evaluation on Apple, Inc's liquidity, let's revisit our conclusions for each of the liquidity ratios:

1. Current and Quick Ratios: Apple is liquid and has more than enough current assets to meet its current financial obligations.

2. Sale-to-Receivables and Days Receivables Ratios: Apple's receivables collection has slowed down in the last 4 years, though the slow down wasn't significant, i.e., an average of a couple of days only.

3. Cash Turnover Ratio: Apple's substantial increase in cash and marketable securities has reduced its ability to use working capital in an efficient manner.

Taking into consideration these liquidity sub-conclusions, we can say that Apple, Inc. is a liquid company with moderate liquidity risk due to slight slowing down in its collection of receivables.

Chapter 5

Profitability

To properly analyze a company's financial performance, i.e., profitability, here are some of the most important ratios to analyze:

1. Gross Profit Margin;

2. Net Profit Margin;

3. Return on Investment;

4. Earnings-per-Share; and

5. Investment Turnover.

Gross Profit Margin

This refers to the difference between the cost of items sold/services delivered and net sales. Also called the spread, the higher the gross profit margin, the better. It's computed by dividing the gross profits over net sales.

So, what are the things that affect the gross profit margin? The two main accounts that affect it are gross profits and net sales.

Gross profits are determined by the selling price/total sales and the cost of the goods sold. When gross profits increase, the gross profit margin increases, too, and vice-versa. To increase gross profits, a company must:

1. Increase its selling price;

2. Reduce the cost of goods sold; or

3. Both.

Net Profit Margin

This gives you an idea of how efficient a company is when it comes to managing its operating expenses. The lesser its expenses are, the greater its net income will be, and the higher its net profit margin will be, too. Assuming the same level of expenses, the higher the net sales are, the higher the net income, too, and the higher the net profit margin will be.

Net profit margin's computed by dividing net income over net sales. The higher the ratio is, the better because the net profit margin indicates how profitable a company is.

Why is the net profit margin important? The ability to improve operational efficiency when it comes to expenses enables a company to increase its profitability even if sales don't grow much. It also makes the impact of increased sales even greater.

Return on Assets

This ratio gives you an idea of how profitable a company's assets are as a whole. It also tells you indirectly how efficient management is in terms of generating net income with the company's assets.

Return on Assets (ROA) is computed by dividing net income over average total assets. The average total assets are computed by adding the ending total assets balance and the previous ending balance and dividing the sum by two as with the gross profit and net profit margins, the higher the number, the better.

As you can see, the two important aspects of ROA are net income and total assets. When total assets increase, ROA goes down and vice-versa. When net income increases, ROA goes up and vice-versa.

Earnings-Per-Share

Also referred to as EPS, it gives you an idea of how much each share of stock of a company has earned for a fiscal year. It's computed by dividing net income after taxes by the total number of shares outstanding as of the end of the fiscal year. The higher the EPS number, the better because it means each share earned more.

Return on Investment

There are two versions of this ratio: from management's perspective and from a stock investor's perspective.

The management perspective of return on investment (ROI) divides net income after taxes over total stockholders' equity. As such, it's often referred to as ROE or return on equity.

On the other hand, the stock investor's perspective on return on investment has two versions:

1. Change in stock price divided by initial or buying price; and

2. EPS divided by the previous year-end stock price.

These are called "stock investors'" perspective because it evaluates profitability based on a stock's EPS and acquisition cost or current market price, instead of total stockholder equity and total net income after taxes, which is the perspective from which a company's management evaluated profitability.

Regardless of the perspective, the higher the number, the better, and vice-versa.

Again, let's use the balance sheet and income statement of Apple, Inc., for consistency:

Apple Inc.

CONSOLIDATED BALANCE SHEETS

For Fiscal Years Ending September 30

In Millions, Except for Fiscal Year-End Stock Prices

	2019	2018	2017	2016	2015
ASSETS:					
Current assets:					
Cash and cash equivalents	$ 48,844.00	$ 25,913.00	$ 20,289.00	$ 20,484.00	$ 21,120.00
Marketable securities	$ 51,713.00	$ 40,388.00	$ 53,892.00	$ 46,671.00	$ 20,481.00
Accounts receivable, net	$ 22,926.00	$ 23,186.00	$ 17,874.00	$ 15,754.00	$ 16,849.00
Inventories	$ 4,106.00	$ 3,956.00	$ 4,855.00	$ 2,132.00	$ 2,349.00
Vendor non-trade receivables	$ 22,878.00	$ 25,809.00	$ 17,799.00	$ 13,545.00	$ 13,494.00
Other current assets	$ 12,352.00	$ 12,087.00	$ 13,936.00	$ 8,283.00	$ 15,085.00
Total current assets	$ 162,819.00	$ 131,339.00	$ 128,645.00	$106,869.00	$ 89,378.00
Non-current assets:					
Marketable securities	$ 105,341.00	$ 170,799.00	$ 194,714.00	$170,430.00	$ 164,065.00
Property, plant and equipment, net	$ 37,378.00	$ 41,304.00	$ 33,783.00	$ 27,010.00	$ 22,471.00
Other non-current assets	$ 32,978.00	$ 22,283.00	$ 18,177.00	$ 17,377.00	$ 14,431.00
Total non-current assets	$ 175,697.00	$ 234,386.00	$ 246,674.00	$ 214,817.00	$ 200,967.00
Total assets	**$ 338,516.00**	**$ 365,725.00**	**$ 375,319.00**	**$321,686.0**	**$ 290,345.00**
LIABILITIES AND SHAREHOLDERS' EQUITY:					
Current liabilities:					
Accounts payable	$ 46,236.00	$ 55,888.00	$ 44,242.00	$ 37,294.00	$ 35,490.00
Other current liabilities	$ 37,720.00	$ 32,687.00	$ 30,551.00	$ 22,027.00	$ 25,181.00
Deferred revenue	$ 5,522.00	$ 7,543.00	$ 7,548.00	$ 8,080.00	$ 8,940.00

Commercial paper	$ 5,980.00	$ 11,964.00	$ 11,977.00	$ 8,105.00	$ 8,499.00
Term debt	$ 10,260.00	$ 8,784.00	$ 6,496.00	$ 3,500.00	$ 2,500.00
Total current liabilities	**$ 105,718.00**	**$ 116,866.00**	**$ 100,814.00**	**$79,006.00**	**$80,610.00**
Non-current liabilities: Deferred revenue		$ 2,797.00	$ 2,836.00	$ 2,930.00	$ 3,624.00
Term debt	$ 91,807.00	$ 93,735.00	$ 97,207.00	$ 75,427.00	$ 53,329.00
Other non-current liabilities	$ 50,503.00	$ 45,180.00	$ 40,415.00	$ 36,074.00	$ 33,427.00
Total non-current liabilities	*$ 142,310.00*	*$ 141,712.00*	*$ 140,458.00*	*$114,431.0*	*$ 90,380.00*
Total liabilities	**$ 248,028.00**	**$258,578.00**	**$ 241,272.00**	**193,437.00**	**$ 170,990.00**
Commitments and contingencies					
Shareholders' equity:					
Common stock and additional paid-in capital, $0.00001 par value: 12,600,000 shares authorized; 4,754,986 and 5,126,201 shares issued and outstanding, respectively	$ 45,174.00	$ 40,201.00	$ 35,867.00	$ 31,251.00	$ 27,416.00
Retained earnings	$ 45,898.00	$ 70,400.00	$ 98,330.00	$ 96,364.00	$ 92,284.00
Accumulated other comprehensive income/(loss)	$ (584.00)	$ (3,454.00)	$ (150.00)	$ 634.00	$ (345.00)
Total shareholders' equity	*$ 90,488.00*	*$ 107,147.00*	*$ 134,047.00*	*$128,249.0*	*$ 119,355.00*
Total liabilities and shareholders' equity	**$ 338,516.00**	**$365,725.00**	**$ 375,319.00**	**$321,686.0**	**$ 290,345.00**
Net Working Capital	**$ 57,101.00**	**$ 14,473.00**	**$ 27,831.00**	**$27,863.00**	**$ 8,768.00**
Fiscal Year-End Stock Prices	**$ 248.02**	**$ 214.87**	**$ 163.49**	**$ 107.91**	**$ 111.19**

Apple, Inc.

CONSOLIDATED STATEMENTS OF OPERATIONS

In millions, except number of shares which are reflected in thousands and per share amounts)

Fiscal Years Ending in September 30

	$ 2,019	$ 2,018	$ 2,017	$ 2,016	$ 2,015
Net sales:					
Products	$ 213,883	$ 225,847	$ 196,534		
Services	$ 46,291	$ 39,748	$ 32,700		
Total net sales	**$ 260,174**	**$ 265,595**	**$ 229,234**	**$ 215,639**	**$ 233,715**
*Theoretical Credit Sales	$ 110,000	$ 150,000	$ 130,000	$ 90,000	$ 120,000
Cost of sales:					
Total cost of sales	*$ 161,782*	*$ 163,756*	*$ 141,048*	*$ 131,376*	*$ 140,089*
Gross margin	**$ 98,392**	**$ 101,839**	**$ 88,186**	**$84,263**	**$ 93,626**
Operating expenses:					
Research and development	$ 16,217	$ 14,236	$ 11,581	$ 10,045	$ 8,067
Selling, general and administrative	$ 18,245	$ 16,705	$ 15,261	$ 14,194	$ 14,329
Total operating expenses	*$ 34,462*	*$ 30,941*	*$ 26,842*	*$ 24,239*	*$ 22,396*
Operating income	**$ 63,930**	**$ 70,898**	**$ 61,344**	**$ 60,024**	**$ 71,230**
Other income/(expense), net	$ 1,807	$ 2,005	$ 2,745	$ 1,348	$ 1,285
Income before provision for income taxes	**$ 65,737**	**$ 72,903**	**$ 64,089**	**$ 61,372**	**$ 72,515**
Provision for income taxes	$ 10,481	$ 13,372	$ 15,738	$ 15,685	$ 19,121
Net income	**$ 55,256**	**$ 59,531**	**$ 48,351**	**$ 45,687**	**$ 53,394**

Earnings per share:

Basic	$ 12	$ 12	$ 9	$ 8	$ 9

Shares used in computing earnings per share:

Basic	$ 4,617,834	$4,955,377	$5,217,242	$5,470,820	$5,753,421

And here are the profitability ratios of the company, too, based on the balance sheet and income statements above:

Profitability Ratios	2019	2018	2017	2016	2015
Gross Profit Margin (Gross Profits/Net Sales)	37.82%	38.34%	38.47%	39.08%	40.06%
Net Profit Margin (Net Income/Net Sales)	21.24%	22.41%	21.09%	21.19%	22.85%
Return on Assets (Net Income/Total Assets)	16.32%	16.28%	12.88%	14.20%	18.39%
Earnings-per-Share (EPS) Net Income/Outstanding Shares	$ 11.97	$ 12.01	$ 9.27	$ 8.35	$ 9.28
Return on investment – Management's View Point (Net Income/Owners' Equity)	47.69%	51.38%	41.73%	39.43%	46.09%
Return on investment – Stock Investor's Viewpoint 1 (Change in Stock Price/Initial Stock Price)	15.43%	31.43%	51.51%	-2.95%	n/a
Return on investment – Stock Investor's Viewpoint 2 (EPS/Previous Year-End Stock Price)	5.57%	7.35%	8.59%	7.51%	5.57%

Let's go through each of the ratios, shall we?

What did you glean from Apple's gross profit margin from 2015 to 2019? First, it has been declining. From 40.06% in 2015 to only 37.82%, that's a 2.24% contraction. Now, that may not sound much, but if you're talking about annual sales of over $200 billion, 2.24% is more than $4 billion of lost gross profits.

Now, it doesn't mean Apple's sales went down since 2015. No, that's not the point of gross profit margin. It's about how much a company has left of its net sales for funding its operations. Gross profit margins are more about spreads or percentages of sales and not actual dollars. And these figures can give you clues on two possible things:

1. The cost of the goods the company is selling is increasing at a faster rate than the rise in their selling prices; or

2. The market has become more competitive for the company's products that it couldn't increase prices and sales enough to exceed the rise in the cost of goods sold.

Second, given it's the 4th straight fiscal year of declining profit margins, we can reasonably conclude that Apple's gross profit margin is at moderate risk of a continuing decline unless the next fiscal year will result in an increase.

Now let's look at the net profit margin. As with the gross profit margin, it has declined to only 21.24% from 2015's 22.85%. What could be the reason for its declining net profitability?

There are two factors that affect net profit margin: net sales and net income. If net profit margin declines, the possible reasons are:

1. Decline in net income while net sales remain the same or increase; or

2. Slower growth in net income compared to the growth of net sales.

In turn, net income is affected by gross profit margin and operating expenses. When the gross profit margin goes down, it can pull down net income. When operating expenses go up, it reduces net income.

If you look at net sales, it went up from 2015 levels by about $26 billion at an average annual rate of 2.72%. And if you remember our analysis of gross profit margin earlier, it went down for four straight years, right? How's that?

The cost of sales grew at an average annual rate of 3.66% compared to only 2.72% for net sales. This is the reason for the declining gross profit margin. And because operating expenses grew at an average annual rate of 11.38% from 2015 to 2019, the net profit margin went down, too. As a result, the net profit margin is at a moderate risk of continued decline.

Looking at return on assets, it has also gone down from 2015 levels, but it has picked up for two straight years already, beginning in the fiscal year 2018. From a ROA of 18.39% in 2015, it bottomed out at 12.88% in 2017 before picking up again in fiscal years 2018 and

2019. This indicates that Apple's assets are starting to become more profitable again.

The company's EPS shows an increasing trend, from only $9.28 per share in 2015 to $11.97 for the fiscal year 2019. This increase puts EPS average annual growth rate at 6.57%. But is it really a case of greater profitability, given the declines in its net profit and gross profit margins?

There are two components that determine EPS, i.e., net income and the total number of shares outstanding. Net income grew at an average annual rate of only 0.86% since 2015, but EPS grew at an average annual growth rate of 6.57%. This means the growth rate for total outstanding shares was way slower than that of net income. And in this case, the total number of outstanding shares of Apple, Inc. actually went down by an average of 5.35% every year. Growth in the numerator (net income) coupled with a decrease in the denominator (shares outstanding) resulted in a higher EPS since 2015.

Despite the growth of EPS over the last 4 years, the risk of a decline in EPS in the next fiscal year or two is moderate. This is because the impressive growth rate was largely due to the substantial decrease in the outstanding number of Apple shares.

Finally, we look at the return on investment ratios, i.e., return on equity (management perspective), return on investments 1 and 2 (stock investors' perspective).

From the management and creditors' perspectives, ROE is very good, with an average annual ROE of 45.06%, with a low of 39.43% in the fiscal year 2016 and a high of 51.38% in the fiscal year 2018. There are two important factors that influence ROE: net income and stockholders' equity balances, including retained earnings or previous years' income that wasn't distributed as dividends.

Net income is trending upwards, albeit at a slow growth rate of only 0.86% annually. Given that the company paid a sizeable chunk of its 2017 and 2018 income as dividends to shareholders, retained earnings decreased by more than $20 billion in the last two fiscal years. Coupled with a growing numerator (net income), ROE has increased over the last two fiscal years.

From the stock investors' perspective, let's look at the first ROI, which is based on capital appreciation, i.e., an increase in stock price. After registering a staggering 51.51% price increase during the fiscal year 2017, Apple's stock price seems to be losing steam as it registered capital appreciation-based returns of only 31.43% and 15.43% in 2018 and 2019, respectively.

One possible reason for the weakening rate of capital appreciation is the fact that Apple's net sales and net income were less than those of the fiscal year 2018. Remember, stock prices are mainly affected by the general investing public's perception of a company's future profitability. Seeing declines in net sales and net income decline this year, coupled with the fact that Apple's losing market share in the smartphone and computer markets in the last two years, can understandably make investors less bullish on its stocks.

Looking at the second ROI, which is dividing the EPS (earnings-per-share) over the previous fiscal year's ending stock price, we see that while it's unchanged compared to the 2015 fiscal year-end levels, it's actually on a downward trend. It achieved a 5-year peak in 2017 at 8.59%, and since then, it has declined in the last two years to 7.35% and 5.57% in fiscal years 2018 and 2019, respectively. Why?

The two main components of the second ROI are EPS and the previous fiscal year-end's stock price. Here's how they affect ROI:

1. An EPS (numerator) increase, assuming the same stock price (denominator), increases the ROI while an EPS decrease reduces the ROI;

2. An increase in the stock price (denominator), assuming EPS remains unchanged, decreases the ROI and vice-versa;

3. A slower EPS growth rate compared to the growth rate at the stock price leads to a lower ROI and vice-versa; and

4. A slower decline in EPS compared to that of the stock prices leads to a higher ROI.

In the case of Apple, Inc., the average annual growth rate in its EPS was much slower than the annual average growth rate of its stock price. Hence, its second ROI has gone down in the last two years.

The two ROI ratios from the stock investors' perspective show that Apple, Inc. is still a profitable stock investment. What it's saying, though, is it's becoming less profitable. Hence, you should also check out the profitability of its peers and industry.

Putting It Together: Profitability

To recap, here are our conclusions for profitability ratios:

1. Gross Profit Margin: Given its 4th straight year of slight declines, the risk of further decline for the next fiscal year or two is moderate.

2. Net Profit Margin: Given the moderate risk of further decline in gross profits and slower growth rate for sales compared to operating expenses, the company's risk for lower net profit margins for the next fiscal year or two is moderate.

3. Return on Assets: Given the increase in ROA over the last two fiscal years, the risk for decline in ROA for the next fiscal year or two is low.

4. Earnings-per-Share (EPS): The Company's per-share profitability has grown substantially but mainly because of the significant reduction in the total number of outstanding shares and given the slow average annual increase in net income, the risk of lower EPS in the next fiscal year or two is low.

5. Return on Equity Investment from Management and Creditors' Perspective (ROE): The Company continues to be a very profitable one with an annual average ROE of 45.06%, and the risk of declining ROE is moderate.

6. Return on Investments (ROI) 1: The company's stock price continues to go up, but it seems to be losing steam, registering a three-year low annual capital appreciation rate of 15.43% due to declining investor sentiment arising from declining gross profit margins and decreasing share of the consumer electronics market. As a result, its risk for a lower ROI 1 in the next fiscal year or two is moderate.

7. Return on Investments (ROI) 2: With a faster average annual growth rate in the price of its stock compared to that of its EPS, ROI continues to decline. As a result, the risk of a lower ROI for the next fiscal year or two is moderate.

Given these financial ratio conclusions, we can conclude that while Apple continues to be a very profitable company from both the management/creditors and stock investors' perspective, its risk for declining profitability in the next fiscal year or two is moderate.

Chapter 6

Operating Efficiency

T his is another important aspect of a company's financial performance. Though its impact isn't as quickly felt or reflected on a company's financials, prolonged inefficiencies can eventually affect its profitability, liquidity, and, eventually, solvency.

The key ratios to consider when evaluating a company's efficiency are:

1. Annual Inventory Turnover Ratio;

2. Inventory Holding Period;

3. Inventory to Assets Ratio;

4. Accounts Receivable Turnover Ratio; and

5. Average Collection Period.

The first three ratios impact profitability and, ultimately, solvency, during the last two impact liquidity.

Using Apple's financial statements again:

Apple Inc.
CONSOLIDATED BALANCE SHEETS
For Fiscal Years Ending September 30
In Millions, Except for Fiscal Year-End Stock Prices

	2019	2018	2017	2016	2015
ASSETS:					
Current assets:					
Cash and cash equivalents	$ 48,844.00	$ 25,913.00	$ 20,289.00	$ 20,484.00	$ 21,120.00
Marketable securities	$ 51,713.00	$ 40,388.00	$ 53,892.00	$ 46,671.00	$ 20,481.00
Accounts receivable, net	$ 22,926.00	$ 23,186.00	$ 17,874.00	$ 15,754.00	$ 16,849.00
Inventories	$ 4,106.00	$ 3,956.00	$ 4,855.00	$ 2,132.00	$ 2,349.00
Average Inventory Levels	$ 4,031.00	$ 4,405.50	$ 3,493.50	$ 2,240.50	N/A
Vendor non-trade receivables	$ 22,878.00	$ 25,809.00	$ 17,799.00	$ 13,545.00	$ 13,494.00
Other current assets	$ 12,352.00	$ 12,087.00	$ 13,936.00	$ 8,283.00	$ 15,085.00
Total current assets	$ 162,819.00	$ 131,339.00	$ 128,645.00	$106,869.00	$ 89,378.00
Non-current assets:					
Marketable securities	$ 105,341.00	$ 170,799.00	$ 194,714.00	$170,430.00	$ 164,065.00
Property, plant and equipment, net	$ 37,378.00	$ 41,304.00	$ 33,783.00	$27,010.00	$ 22,471.00
Other non-current assets	$ 32,978.00	$ 22,283.00	$ 18,177.00	$ 17,377.00	$ 14,431.00
Total non-current assets	$ 175,697.00	$ 234,386.00	$ 246,674.00	$ 214,817.00	$ 200,967.00
Total assets	**$ 338,516.00**	**$365,725.00**	**$ 375,319.00**	**$321,686.0**	**$ 290,345.00**
LIABILITIES AND SHAREHOLDERS' EQUITY:					
Current liabilities:					
Accounts payable	$ 46,236.00	$ 55,888.00	$ 44,242.00	$ 37,294.00	$ 35,490.00
Other current liabilities	$ 37,720.00	$ 32,687.00	$ 30,551.00	$ 22,027.00	$ 25,181.00
Deferred revenue	$ 5,522.00	$ 7,543.00	$ 7,548.00	$ 8,080.00	$ 8,940.00
Commercial paper	$ 5,980.00	$ 11,964.00	$ 11,977.00	$ 8,105.00	$ 8,499.00

Term debt	$ 10,260.00	$ 8,784.00	$ 6,496.00	$ 3,500.00	$ 2,500.00
Total current liabilities	**$ 105,718.00**	**$ 116,866.00**	**$ 100,814.00**	**79,006.00**	**$ 80,610.00**
Non-current liabilities:					
Deferred revenue		$ 2,797.00	$ 2,836.00	$ 2,930.00	$ 3,624.00
Term debt	$ 91,807.00	$ 93,735.00	$ 97,207.00	$ 75,427.00	$ 53,329.00
Other non-current liabilities	$ 50,503.00	$ 45,180.00	$ 40,415.00	$ 36,074.00	$ 33,427.00
Total non-current liabilities	***$ 142,310.00***	***$ 141,712.00***	***$ 140,458.00***	***$114,431.0***	***$ 90,380.00***
Total liabilities	**$ 248,028.00**	**$258,578.00**	**$ 241,272.00**	**$193,437.0**	**$ 170,990.00**
Commitments and contingencies					
Shareholders' equity:					
Common stock and additional paid-in capital, $0.00001 par value: 12,600,000 shares authorized; 4,754,986 and 5,126,201 shares issued and outstanding, respectively	$ 45,174.00	$ 40,201.00	$ 35,867.00	$ 31,251.00	$ 27,416.00
Retained earnings	$ 45,898.00	$ 70,400.00	$ 98,330.00	$ 96,364.00	$ 92,284.00
Accumulated other comprehensive income/(loss)	$ (584.00)	$ (3,454.00)	$ (150.00)	$ 634.00	$ (345.00)
Total shareholders' equity	***$ 90,488.00***	***$ 107,147.00***	***$ 134,047.00***	***$128,249.0***	***$ 119,355.00***
Total liabilities and shareholders' equity	**$ 338,516.00**	**$365,725.00**	**$ 375,319.00**	**$321,686.0**	**$ 290,345.00**
Net Working Capital	**$ 57,101.00**	**$ 14,473.00**	**$ 27,831.00**	**$27,863.00**	**$ 8,768.00**
Fiscal Year-End Stock Prices	**$ 248.02**	**$ 214.87**	**$ 163.49**	**$ 107.91**	**$ 111.19**

Apple, Inc.
CONSOLIDATED STATEMENTS OF OPERATIONS
In millions, except number of shares which are reflected
in thousands and per share amounts)

Fiscal Years Ending in September 30

	$ 2,019	$ 2,018	$ 2,017	$ 2,016	$ 2,015
Net sales:					
Products	$ 213,883	$ 225,847	$ 196,534		
Services	$ 46,291	$ 39,748	$ 32,700		
Total net sales	**$ 260,174**	**$ 265,595**	**$ 229,234**	**$ 215,639**	**$ 233,715**
*Theoretical Credit Sales	$ 110,000	$ 150,000	$ 130,000	$ 90,000	$ 120,000
Cost of sales:					
Total cost of sales	*$ 161,782*	*$ 163,756*	*$ 141,048*	*$ 131,376*	*$ 140,089*
Gross margin	**$ 98,392**	**$ 101,839**	**$ 88,186**	**$ 84,263**	**$ 93,626**
Operating expenses:					
Research and development	$ 16,217	$ 14,236	$ 11,581	$ 10,045	$ 8,067
Selling, general and administrative	$ 18,245	$ 16,705	$ 15,261	$ 14,194	$ 14,329
Total operating expenses	*$ 34,462*	*$ 30,941*	*$ 26,842*	*$ 24,239*	*$ 22,396*
Operating income	**$ 63,930**	**$ 70,898**	**$ 61,344**	**$ 60,024**	**$ 71,230**
Other income/(expense), net	$ 1,807	$ 2,005	$ 2,745	$ 1,348	$ 1,285
Income before provision for income taxes	**$ 65,737**	**$ 72,903**	**$ 64,089**	**$ 61,372**	**$ 72,515**
Provision for income taxes	$ 10,481	$ 13,372	$ 15,738	$ 15,685	$ 19,121
Net income	**$ 55,256**	**$ 59,531**	**$ 48,351**	**$ 45,687**	**$ 53,394**
Earnings per share:					
Basic	$ 12	$ 12	$ 9	$ 8	$ 9
Shares used in computing earnings per share:					
Basic	$ 4,617,834	$4,955,377	$5,217,242	$5,470,820	$5,753,421

Here are Apple's key efficiency ratios:

Efficiency Ratios	2019	2018	2017	2016	2015
Annual inventory turnover (Cost of Goods Sold for the Year/Average Inventory)	40.13	37.17	40.37	58.64	59.64
Inventory holding period (365/Annual Inventory Turnover)	9.09	9.82	9.04	6.22	6.12
Inventory to assets ratio (Inventory/Total Assets)	1.21%	1.08%	1.29%	0.66%	0.81%
Accounts receivable turnover [Net (credit) Sales/Average Accounts Receivable]	4.77	7.31	7.73	5.52	7.12
Collection period (365/Accounts Receivable Turnover)	76.50	49.96	47.21	66.11	51.25

So, how efficient is Apple, Inc.?

Let's look at the inventory turnover first. The inventory turnover ratio tells you how many times during the fiscal year, the company turns over its inventories, i.e., how many times it empties and replenishes it. The higher the number, the more times a company turns over its inventories, which indicates brisk sales vis-a-vis inventory stocking. Lower numbers mean slower sales vis-a-vis inventory stocking.

Since 2015, inventory turnover has slowed down from 59.64 times to only 40.13 times during the fiscal year. There are two important components of inventory turnover: cost of goods sold for the fiscal year and average inventory levels. These two impact a company's inventory turnovers in the following ways:

1. Assuming average inventory levels remain unchanged, an increase in the cost of goods sold increases inventory turnover and vice-versa; and

2. Assuming the cost of goods sold stay the same, an increase in average inventory levels decreases inventory turnover and vice-versa.

Looking at the income statement, you can see that the cost of goods sold has increased from the fiscal year 2015 to 2019 at an average annual rate of 3.66%. Looking at the balance sheet, you can see that average inventories have also increased from the fiscal year 2016 to 2019 at an average annual growth rate of 21.62%.

Because growth in average inventories was a lot faster than growth in sales, particularly the cost of goods sold, the net effect was slower inventory turnover at only 40.13 times in the fiscal year 2019 compared to 59.64 times during the fiscal year 2015. This tells us that Apple's ability to dispose of its inventories declined.

The decline in such ability is also reflected in its average inventory holding period, which is primarily affected by inventory turnover. The slower turnover indicates that, on average, Apple held on to its inventories during the fiscal year 2019 for an average of 9.09 days compared to only 6.12 days during the fiscal year 2015.

These aren't surprising considering the aggressive campaigns mounted by major Chinese electronic brands like Huawei, Xiaomi, Oppo, and Vivo. During the third quarter of 2015, Apple had the second-highest global market share of smartphones at 13.4%, trailing only Samsung's 23.3% share, according to statistica.com. But as of the third quarter of 2019, Apple's market share stayed at 13%, but top Chinese brand Huawei cornered 18.6% of the global smartphone market share. As a result, Huawei is now the second-biggest smartphone manufacturer in the world while Apple dropped to the third spot. Clearly, increasing competition from top Chinese brands and a growing number of complaints about the newer iPhone models are already slowing down the company's ability to dispose of its inventories.

We can also see this in the company's inventory to assets ratio, which has gone up from 0.81% as of fiscal year ending September 2015 to 1.21% as of September 2019. Slower sales growth compared to inventory growth has increased the portion of the company's assets in inventories. Fortunately, it's just a very small amount and isn't a concern as of now.

Let's take a look at the other aspect of the company's efficiency, i.e., collection of receivables. For this, we turn to the accounts receivable turnover ratio and average collection period.

Looking at the accounts receivable turnover, we can see that it went down from 7.12 times in the fiscal year 2015 to only 4.77 times in the fiscal year 2019. This means it collects on its entire accounts receivables 4.77 times during the fiscal year 2019 compared to 7.12 times during the fiscal year 2015, which indicates a longer receivables collection period.

This is evident in its average collection period, which increased to 76.50 days during 2019 from only 51.25 days in 2015. Either the company relaxed its collection policies, or it has a harder time collecting from its distributors/customers. Either way, longer collection periods mean it takes longer for credit sales-related cash to come in, which can contribute to higher liquidity risk.

Putting It Together: Operating Efficiency

Let's get a summary of our conclusions for each of the key operating efficiency ratios we analyzed:

1. Inventory Turnover Ratio: Inventory turnover slowed down due because growth in average inventory was faster compared to average growth in sales, particularly the cost of goods sold. This indicates that Apple is having an increasingly challenging time moving its inventories, probably due to more intense competition from top Chinese electronic brands like Huawei, Xiaomi, Oppo, and Vivo.

2. Average Inventory Holding Period: The increase in the average number of days Apple holds on to its inventories increased from 2015 because of lower inventory turnovers brought about by aggressive campaigns launched by top Chinese electronic brands, which demoted Apple to third place in global market share for smartphones.

3. Inventory to Assets Ratio: As the speed at which the company's ability to move its inventories slowed down, it wasn't surprising to see a slight increase in the proportion of its total assets held in inventories. This isn't anything to be

concerned about as, despite the increase, inventories comprise a mere 1.21% of total assets only.

4. Receivables Turnover Ratio: The slowdown in its receivables turnover ratio may indicate a relaxing of receivables collection policies in light of heightened competition or clients having a harder time selling Apple products, which affect their ability to pay the company back on time.

5. Average Receivables Collection Period: The 25-day increase in average collection period from only 51.25 days in 2015 to 76.50 days in 2019 was mainly due to lower receivables turnover, which was most likely caused by increased competition from top Chinese electronic brands like Huawei.

Given the conclusions on the above-mentioned operating efficiency ratios, we can conclude that:

1. Apple's operating efficiency is declining both in terms of moving inventories and collecting receivables;

2. Its risk of further operating efficiency declines is moderate, considering the stiffer competition coming from top Chinese brands; and

3. The decline in inventory turnover may be a contributing factor to its declining profitability, too.

Chapter 7

Solvency

If liquidity refers to a company's ability to meet its current or short-term financial obligations, solvencies about its ability to meet long-term debts or financial obligations. By long-term, we mean financial obligations or debts that are due after 12 months or one year.

A company continues to remain solvent for as long as the total book value of its assets is greater than its liabilities. The moment that liabilities exceed the total book value of assets, the company becomes insolvent or bankrupt.

The key ratios for evaluating solvency are:

1. Debt to Equity Ratio;

2. Debt to Total Assets Ratio; and

3. Interest Coverage Ratio.

Using Apple's financial statements, let's compute its solvency ratios and evaluate the company's solvency, shall we?

Apple Inc.

CONSOLIDATED BALANCE SHEETS

For Fiscal Years Ending September 30

In Millions, Except for Fiscal Year-End Stock Prices

	<u>2019</u>	<u>2018</u>	<u>2017</u>	<u>2016</u>	<u>2015</u>
ASSETS:					
Current assets:					
Cash and cash equivalents	$ 48,844.00	$ 25,913.00	$ 20,289.00	$ 20,484.00	$ 21,120.00
Marketable securities	$ 51,713.00	$ 40,388.00	$ 53,892.00	$ 46,671.00	$ 20,481.00
Accounts receivable, net	$ 22,926.00	$ 23,186.00	$ 17,874.00	$ 15,754.00	$ 16,849.00
Inventories	$ 4,106.00	$ 3,956.00	$ 4,855.00	$ 2,132.00	$ 2,349.00
Average Inventory Levels	$ 4,031.00	$ 4,405.50	$ 3,493.50	$ 2,240.50	N/A
Vendor non-trade receivables	$ 22,878.00	$ 25,809.00	$ 17,799.00	$ 13,545.00	$ 13,494.00
Other current assets	$ 12,352.00	$ 12,087.00	$ 13,936.00	$ 8,283.00	$ 15,085.00
Total current assets	$ 162,819.00	$ 131,339.00	$ 128,645.00	$106,869.00	$ 89,378.00
Non-current assets:					
Marketable securities	$ 105,341.00	$ 170,799.00	$ 194,714.00	$170,430.00	$ 164,065.00
Property, plant and equipment, net	$ 37,378.00	$ 41,304.00	$ 33,783.00	$ 27,010.00	$ 22,471.00
Other non-current assets	$ 32,978.00	$ 22,283.00	$ 18,177.00	$ 17,377.00	$ 14,431.00
Total non-current assets	$ 175,697.00	$ 234,386.00	$ 246,674.00	$ 214,817.00	$ 200,967.00
Total assets	**$ 338,516.00**	**$ 365,725.00**	**$ 375,319.00**	**$321,686.00**	**$ 290,345.00**
LIABILITIES AND SHAREHOLDERS' EQUITY:					
Current liabilities:					
Accounts payable	$ 46,236.00	$ 55,888.00	$ 44,242.00	$ 37,294.00	$ 35,490.00
Other current liabilities	$ 37,720.00	$ 32,687.00	$ 30,551.00	$ 22,027.00	$ 25,181.00
Deferred revenue	$ 5,522.00	$ 7,543.00	$ 7,548.00	$ 8,080.00	$ 8,940.00
Commercial paper	$ 5,980.00	$ 11,964.00	$ 11,977.00	$ 8,105.00	$ 8,499.00
Term debt	$ 10,260.00	$ 8,784.00	$ 6,496.00	$ 3,500.00	$ 2,500.00

Total current liabilities	$ 105,718.00	$ 116,866.00	$ 100,814.00	$79,006.00	$ 80,610.00
Non-current liabilities:					
Deferred revenue		$ 2,797.00	$ 2,836.00	$ 2,930.00	$ 3,624.00
Term debt	$ 91,807.00	$ 93,735.00	$ 97,207.00	$ 75,427.00	$ 53,329.00
Other non-current liabilities	$ 50,503.00	$ 45,180.00	$ 40,415.00	$ 36,074.00	$ 33,427.00
Total non-current liabilities	*$ 142,310.00*	*$ 141,712.00*	*$ 140,458.00*	*$114,431.0*	*$ 90,380.00*
Total liabilities	**$ 248,028.00**	**$ 258,578.00**	**$ 241,272.00**	**$193,437.0**	**$ 170,990.00**
Commitments and contingencies					
Shareholders' equity:					
Common stock and additional paid-in capital, $0.00001 par value: 12,600,000 shares authorized; 4,754,986 and 5,126,201 shares issued and outstanding, respectively	$ 45,174.00	$ 40,201.00	$ 35,867.00	$ 31,251.00	$ 27,416.00
Retained earnings	$ 45,898.00	$ 70,400.00	$ 98,330.00	$ 96,364.00	$ 92,284.00
Accumulated other comprehensive income/(loss)	$ (584.00)	$ (3,454.00)	$ (150.00)	$ 634.00	$ (345.00)
Total shareholders' equity	*$ 90,488.00*	*$ 107,147.00*	*$ 134,047.00*	*$128,249.0*	*$ 119,355.00*
Total liabilities and shareholders' equity	**$ 338,516.00**	**$ 365,725.00**	**$ 375,319.00**	**$321,686.0**	**$ 290,345.00**
Net Working Capital	**$ 57,101.00**	**$ 14,473.00**	**$ 27,831.00**	**$27,863.00**	**$ 8,768.00**
Fiscal Year-End Stock Prices	**$ 248.02**	**$ 214.87**	**$ 163.49**	**$ 107.91**	**$ 111.19**

Here are the solvency ratios derived from the company's balance sheet:

Solvency Ratios	2019	2018	2017	2016	2015
Debt to equity ratio (Debt/ Owners' Equity)	274.10%	241.33%	179.99%	150.83%	143.26%
Debt ratio (Debt/Total Assets)	73.27%	70.70%	64.28%	60.13%	58.89%

Looking at the company's debt-to-equity ratio, we can see that since 2015, the percentage of debt in proportion to capital has almost doubled from only 143% as of end of fiscal year 2015 to 274% as of end of fiscal year 2019. What's the reason for this?

The two components of this ratio are total debt and owner's or stockholders' equity. Their impact on solvency is as follows:

1. Assuming stockholders' equity remains the same, an increase in total debt will result in a higher debt to equity ratio and vice-versa; and

2. Assuming total debt stays the same, an increase in stockholders' equity will result in a lower debt-to-equity ratio and vice versa.

Looking at the balance sheet, you'll see that total debts went up to $142 billion during fiscal year 2019 from only $171 billion in 2015, for an average annual growth rate of 13.20%. Stockholders' equity, on the hand, went down to $90.48 billion in fiscal year 2019 from $119.35 billion at the end of fiscal year 2015. Why did stockholders' equity go down?

The balance sheet reveals why. It wasn't due to losses, as the company continued to make lots of money. It paid out retained earnings by way of dividends to its shareholders, particularly in 2018 and 2019, amounting to $27.9 billion and $24.5 billion, respectively.

Therefore, the increase in its debt-to-equity ratio isn't something to be concerned about. The risk of further increase in this ratio is low given the increase was a result of a strategic move by management.

Looking at the company's debt ratio, you'll see that it has gone up by 14 percentage points from end of fiscal year 2015's 58.89% to 73.27% at the end of fiscal year 2019. In the last four years, debt ratio has consistently gone up at an annual average rate of 5.61%. What's the reason for this?

The key components of debt ratio are total debts and total assets. Their effects on debt ratio are as follows:

1. Assuming total assets remain constant, an increase in total debts will increase the debt ratio, and vice-versa; and

2. Assuming total debts remain constant, an increase in total assets will decrease the debt ratio, and vice-versa.

Total debts grew at an average annual rate of 13.20% while total assets grew at an average annual rate of only 3.91%. This means a big chunk of its debts went to finance operations rather than assets.

What does this tell us? It may indicate that the company's increasing average days' receivables (longer time to collect on credit sales) may be forcing the company to borrow more money.

It may also be a strategy to improve the return on investment on its shares of stocks. How?

Debts can drastically reduce the need for additional capital to increase net income. That's why they're called "leverage". While the interest expense on additional debts can take a sizeable chunk of the additional operating income they can help generate, they can still increase total net income, if used wisely.

A higher net income vis-a-vis relatively steady or reduced stockholder's equity will result in a higher return on equity investment. Let me illustrate.

	Scenario A	Scenario B	Scenario C
Total Debts	$50,000.00	$60,000.00	$70,000.00
Total Stockholders' Equity	$20,000.00	$20,000.00	$20,000.00
Net Income	$10,000.00	$11,000.00	$12,000.00
Return on Equity Investment (Net Income ÷ Stockholders' Equity)	**50.00%**	**55.00%**	**60.00%**

This makes sense as the company's return on equity investments have increased from fiscal year 2015 to fiscal year 2019. The significant increase in the company's leverage, i.e., total debts, seems to be a strategic move to improve profitability.

Putting It Together: Solvency

Apple, Inc. remains solvent and given its position in the international consumer electronics market, profitability, and efficiency, risk of insolvency in the near to medium-term is very low.

Chapter 8

Financial Statement
Analysis Case Studies

In this chapter, we'll apply the lessons on financial statement analysis we learned in Chapters 4 to 7 on hypothetical companies. The first of which is Vector Feeds, Inc.

Case Study #1: Vector Feeds, Inc.

Vector Feeds, Inc. is a livestock feeds manufacturing and marketing company. Its market is both local (US) and international, with bulk of their sales coming from the international markets.

Vector Feeds, Inc. (VFI) is one of the country's biggest livestock feeds manufacturers, taking up 35% of the market. Its main market, the livestock growers' industry, forecasts an average annual growth rate for the international livestock industry of 15% for the next 5 years and 10% for the US market. This is good news for companies like VFI as more demand for livestock means more demand – and sales – of livestock feeds.

The following are the company's financial statements, i.e., balance sheet and income statement.

Vector Feeds, Inc.

CONSOLIDATED BALANCE SHEETS

In Millions, Except for Fiscal Year-End Stock Prices

	2019	2018	2017	2016	2015
ASSETS:					
Current assets:					
Cash and cash equivalents	$ 139.55	$ 74.04	$ 57.97	$ 58.53	$ 60.34
Marketable securities	$ 147.75	$ 115.39	$ 153.98	$ 133.35	$ 58.52
Accounts receivable, net	$ 65.50	$ 66.25	$ 51.07	$ 45.01	$ 48.14
Inventories	$ 11.73	$ 11.30	$ 13.87	$ 6.09	$ 6.71
Average Inventory Levels	$ 11.52	$ 12.59	$ 9.98	$ 6.40	#VALUE!
Vendor non-trade receivables	$ 65.37	$ 73.74	$ 50.85	$ 38.70	$ 38.55
Other current assets	$ 35.29	$ 34.53	$ 39.82	$ 23.67	$ 43.10
Total current assets	*$ 465.20*	*$ 375.25*	*$ 367.56*	*$ 305.34*	*$ 255.37*
Non-current assets:					
Marketable securities	$ 300.97	$ 488.00	$ 556.33	$ 486.94	$ 468.76
Property, plant and equipment, net	$ 106.79	$ 118.01	$ 96.52	$ 77.17	$ 64.20
Other non-current assets	$ 94.22	$ 63.67	$ 51.93	$ 49.65	$ 41.23
Total non-current assets	*$ 501.99*	*$ 669.67*	*$ 704.78*	*$ 613.76*	*$ 574.19*
Total assets	**$ 967.19**	**$ 1,044.93**	**$ 1,072.34**	**$ 919.10**	**$ 829.56**
LIABILITIES AND SHAREHOLDERS' EQUITY:					
Current liabilities:					
Accounts payable	$ 132.10	$ 159.68	$ 126.41	$ 106.55	$ 101.40
Other current liabilities	$ 107.77	$ 93.39	$ 87.29	$ 62.93	$ 71.95
Deferred revenue	$ 15.78	$ 21.55	$ 21.57	$ 23.09	$ 25.54

Commercial paper	$ 17.09	$ 34.18	$ 34.22	$ 23.16	$ 24.28
Term debt	$ 29.31	$ 25.10	$ 18.56	$ 10.00	$ 7.14
Total current liabilities	**$ 302.05**	**$ 333.90**	**$ 288.04**	**$ 225.73**	**$ 230.31**
Non-current liabilities:					
Deferred revenue	$ -	$ 7.99	$ 8.10	$ 8.37	$ 10.35
Term debt	$ 262.31	$ 267.81	$ 277.73	$ 215.51	$ 152.37
Other non-current liabilities	$ 144.29	$ 129.09	$ 115.47	$ 103.07	$ 95.51
Total non-current liabilities	*$ 406.60*	*$ 404.89*	*$ 401.31*	*$ 326.95*	*$ 258.23*
Total liabilities	**$ 708.65**	**$ 738.79**	**$ 689.35**	**$ 552.68**	**$ 488.54**
Shareholders' equity:					
Common stock and additional paid-in capital, $0.00001 par value: 12,600,000 shares authorized; 4,754,986 and 5,126,201 shares issued and outstanding, respectively	$ 129.07	$ 114.86	$ 102.48	$ 89.29	$ 78.33
Retained earnings	$ 131.14	$ 201.14	$ 280.94	$ 275.33	$ 263.67
Accumulated other comprehensive income/(loss)	$ (1.67)	$ (9.87)	$ (0.43)	$ 1.81	$ (0.99)
Total shareholders' equity	*$ 258.54*	*$ 306.13*	*$ 382.99*	*$ 366.43*	*$ 341.01*
Total liabilities and shareholders' equity	**$ 967.19**	**$ 1,044.93**	**$ 1,072.34**	**$ 919.10**	**$ 829.56**
	$ 70.01	$ 79.80			
Net Working Capital	**$ 163.15**	**$ 41.35**	**$ 79.52**	**$ 79.61**	**$ 25.05**
Fiscal Year-End Stock Prices	**$ 7.09**	**$ 6.14**	**$ 4.67**	**$ 3.08**	**$ 3.18**

Vector Feeds, Inc.
CONSOLIDATED STATEMENTS OF OPERATIONS
In millions, except number of shares which are reflected in thousands and per share amounts)

	2019	2018	2017	2016	2015
Net sales:					
Total net sales	*$ 743*	*$ 759*	*$ 655*	*$ 616*	*$ 668*
*Theoretical Credit Sales	$ 314	$ 429	$ 371	$ 257	$ 343
Cost of sales:					
Total cost of sales	*$ 462*	*$ 468*	*$ 403*	*$ 375*	*$ 400*
Gross margin	$ 281	$ 291	$ 252	$ 241	$ 268
Operating expenses:					
Research and development	$ 46	$ 41	$ 33	$ 29	$ 23
Selling, general and administrative	$ 52	$ 48	$ 44	$ 41	$ 41
Total operating expenses	*$ 98*	*$ 88*	*$ 77*	*$ 69*	*$ 64*
Operating income	$ 183	$ 203	$ 175	$ 171	$ 204
Other income/(expense), net	$ 5	$ 6	$ 8	$ 4	$ 4
Income before provision for income taxes	$ 188	$ 208	$ 183	$ 175	$ 207
Provision for income taxes	$ 30	$ 38	$ 45	$ 45	$ 55
Net income	$ 158	$ 170	$ 138	$ 131	$ 153
Earnings per share:					
Basic	$ 0.34	$ 0.34	$ 0.26	$ 0.24	$ 0.27
Shares used in computing earnings per share:					
Basic	13,193.81	14,158.22	14,906.41	15,630.91	16,438.35

Given the financial statements above:

1. Compute the following liquidity ratios for each year and draw conclusions from each ratio before making a general conclusion about liquidity:

   - Current Ratio;

   - Quick Ratio;

   - Sales-to-Receivables Ratio; and

   - Days' Receivables.

Liquidity Ratios	2019	2018	2017	2016	2015
Current Ratio (Current Assets/ Current Liabilities)					
Quick Ratio Quick Assets (cash, marketable securities, and receivables)/Current Liabilities					
Sales-to-Receivables (Turnover) Ratio (Net Sales/Accounts Receivable)					
Days' Receivables (365/Sales to receivables ratio)					
Cash Turnover Ratio (Net Sales/ Net Working Capital)					

2. Compute the following profitability ratios for each year and draw conclusions from each ratio before making a general conclusion about profitability:

- Gross Profit Margin;

- Net Profit Margin;

- Return on Assets;

- Earnings-per-Share (EPS);

- Return on Equity Investments (Management's and Creditors' perspective); and

- Return on Investment 1 (i.e., capital appreciation).

Profitability Ratios	2019	2018	2017	2016	2015
Gross Profit Margin (Gross Profits/Net Sales)					
Net Profit Margin (Net Income/Net Sales)					
Return on Assets (Net Income/Total Assets)					
Earnings-per-Share (EPS) Net Income/Outstanding Shares					
Return on Equity Investment Management's and Creditors' Perspective (Net Income/Owners' Equity)					
Return on Investment – Stock Investor's Perspective 1 (Stock Price Change/Previous Period's Ending Stock Price)					
Return on Investment – Stock Investor's Perspective 2 (EPS/Current Stock Price)					

3. Compute the following operating efficiency ratios for each year and draw conclusions from each ratio before making a general conclusion about operating efficiency:

- Inventory Turnover Ratio;

- Average Inventory Holding Period;

- Inventory-to-Assets Ratio;

- Accounts Receivable Turnover; and

- Average Collection Period.

Operating Efficiency Ratios	2019	2018	2017	2016	2015
Annual inventory turnover (Cost of Goods Sold for the Year/Average Inventory)					
Inventory holding period (365/Annual Inventory Turnover)					
Inventory to assets ratio (Inventory/Total Assets)					
Accounts receivable turnover [Net (credit) Sales/Average Accounts Receivable]					
Collection period (365/Accounts Receivable Turnover)					

4. Compute the following solvency ratios for each year and draw conclusions from each ratio before making a general conclusion about solvency:

- Debt-to-Equity Ratio; and

- Debt Ratio.

5. Make a general conclusion about the financial health and performance of Vector Feeds, Inc., including its medium-term prospects.

6. If Vector Feeds, Inc. comes to you to borrow money for expanding its operations, will you or will you not lend to them? Why or why not, and use the results of your financial analysis to support your decision.

Case Study #2: Genius Learning Institute, Inc.

Genius Learning Institute, Inc. (GLII) is one of the biggest technical skills training companies in the United States, and is widely considered to be on the cutting edge of most computer and electronics-related vocational or technical courses.

As more companies eschew college degrees for actual, hands-on experiences and technical skills, industry analysts forecast an average annual growth of 15% for the technical skills training niche in the US for the next 5 years.

Here are GLII's financial statements, from which you can compute financial ratios and evaluate the company's medium-term prospects.

Given the financial statements above:

1. Compute the following liquidity ratios for each year and draw conclusions from each ratio before making a general conclusion about liquidity:

    - Current Ratio;

    - Quick Ratio;

    - Sales-to-Receivables Ratio; and

    - Days' Receivables.

Liquidity Ratios	2019	2018	2017	2016	2015
Current Ratio (Current Assets/Current Liabilities)					
Quick Ratio Quick Assets (cash, marketable securities, and receivables)/Current Liabilities					
Sales-to-Receivables (Turnover) Ratio (Net Sales/Accounts Receivable)					
Days' Receivables (365/Sales to receivables ratio)					
Cash Turnover Ratio (Net Sales/Net Working Capital)					

2. Compute the following profitability ratios for each year and draw conclusions from each ratio before making a general conclusion about profitability:

- Net Profit Margin;

- Return on Assets;

- Earnings-per-Share (EPS);

- Return on Equity Investments (Management's and Creditors' perspective); and

- Return on Investment 1 (i.e., capital appreciation).

Profitability Ratios	2019	2018	2017	2016	2015
Net Profit Margin (Net Income/Net Sales)					
Return on Assets (Net Income/Total Assets)					
Earnings-per-Share (EPS) Net Income/Outstanding Shares					
Return on Equity Investment Management's and Creditors' Perspective (Net Income/Owners' Equity)					
Return on Investment – Stock Investor's Perspective 1 (Stock Price Change/Previous Period's Ending Stock Price)					
Return on Investment – Stock Investor's Perspective 2 (EPS/Current Stock Price)					

3. Compute the following operating efficiency ratios for each year and draw conclusions from each ratio before making a general conclusion about operating efficiency:

- Accounts Receivable Turnover; and

- Average Collection Period.

Operating Efficiency Ratios	2019	2018	2017	2016	2015
Accounts receivable turnover [Net (credit) Sales/Average Accounts Receivable]					
Collection period (365/Accounts Receivable Turnover)					

4. Compute the following solvency ratios for each year and draw conclusions from each ratio before making a general conclusion about solvency:

- Debt-to-Equity Ratio; and

- Debt Ratio.

5. Make a general conclusion about the financial health and performance of Genius Learning Institute, Inc., including its medium-term prospects.

6. If Genius Learning Institute, Inc. comes to you to borrow money for expanding its operations, will you or will you not

lend to them? Why or why not, and use the results of your financial analysis to support your decision.

7. If Genius Learning Institute, Inc. comes to you for additional capital for expanding operations, will you or will you not put in money into the company? Support your decision using the financial statement analysis you conducted.

Case Study #3: Sweet Tooth, Inc.

Sweet Tooth, Inc. (STI) is a large chocolates and candies manufacturing firm with international operations. Its market leadership position puts it in the top five candy and chocolate makers in the world.

Here are STI's financial statements:

Sweet Tooth, Inc.

CONSOLIDATED BALANCE SHEETS

In Millions, Except for Fiscal Year-End Stock Prices

	September 28, 2019	September 29, 2018	September 30, 2017	September 24, 2016
ASSETS:				
Current assets:				
Cash and cash equivalents	$ 24.42	$ 12.96	$ 8.12	$ 8.19
Marketable securities	$ 25.86	$ 20.19	$ 21.56	$ 18.67
Accounts receivable, net	$ 11.46	$ 11.59	$ 7.15	$ 6.30
Inventories	$ 2.05	$ 1.98	$ 1.94	$ 0.85
Average Inventory Levels	$ 2.02	$ 2.20	$ 1.75	$ 1.12
Vendor non-trade receivables	$ 11.44	$ 12.90	$ 7.12	$ 5.42
Other current assets	$ 6.18	$ 6.04	$ 5.57	$ 3.31
Total current assets	*$ 81.41*	*$ 65.67*	*$ 51.46*	*$ 42.75*
Non-current assets:				
Marketable securities	$ 52.67	$ 85.40	$ 77.89	$ 68.17
Property, plant and equipment, net	$ 18.69	$ 20.65	$ 13.51	$ 10.80
Other non-current assets	$ 16.49	$ 11.14	$ 7.27	$ 6.95
Total non-current assets	*$ 87.85*	*$ 117.19*	*$ 98.67*	*$ 85.93*
Total assets	**$ 169.26**	**$ 182.86**	**$ 150.13**	**$ 128.67**

		$ -	$ -

LIABILITIES AND SHAREHOLDERS' EQUITY:

Current liabilities:

Accounts payable	$ 23.12	$ 27.94	$ 17.70	$ 14.92
Other current liabilities	$ 18.86	$ 16.34	$ 12.22	$ 8.81
Deferred revenue	$ 2.76	$ 3.77	$ 3.02	$ 3.23
Commercial paper	$ 2.99	$ 5.98	$ 4.79	$ 3.24
Term debt	$ 5.13	$ 4.39	$ 2.60	$ 1.40
Total current liabilities	**$ 52.86**	**$ 58.43**	**$ 40.33**	**$ 31.60**

Non-current liabilities:

Deferred revenue	$ -	$ 1.40	$ 1.13	$ 1.17
Term debt	$ 45.90	$ 46.87	$ 38.88	$ 30.17
Other non-current liabilities	$ 25.25	$ 22.59	$ 16.17	$ 14.43
Total non-current liabilities	***$ 71.16***	***$ 70.86***	***$ 56.18***	***$ 45.77***
Total liabilities	**$ 124.01**	**$ 129.29**	**$ 96.51**	**$ 77.37**

Shareholders' equity:	$ -	$ -	$ -	$ -
Common stock and additional paid-in capital, $0.00001	$ -	$ -	$ -	$ -
par value: 12,600,000 shares authorized; 4,754,986 and	$ -	$ -	$ -	$ -
5,126,201 shares issued and outstanding, respectively	$ 22.59	$ 20.10	$ 14.35	$ 12.50
Retained earnings	$ 22.95	$ 35.20	$ 39.33	$ 38.55
Accumulated other comprehensive income/(loss)	$ (0.29)	$ (1.73)	$ (0.06)	$ 0.25
Total shareholders' equity	***$ 45.24***	***$ 53.57***	***$ 53.62***	***$ 51.30***
Total liabilities and shareholders' equity	**$ 169.26**	**$ 182.86**	**$ 150.13**	**$ 128.67**
Net Working Capital	**$ 28.55**	**$ 7.24**	**$ 11.13**	**$ 11.15**
Fiscal Year-End Stock Prices	**$ 7.09**	**$ 6.14**	**$ 4.67**	**$ 3.08**

Given the financial statements above:

1. Compute the following liquidity ratios for each year and draw conclusions from each ratio before making a general conclusion about liquidity:

   - Current Ratio;

   - Quick Ratio;

   - Sales-to-Receivables Ratio; and

   - Days' Receivables.

Liquidity Ratios	2019	2018	2017	2016
Current Ratio (Current Assets/ Current Liabilities)				
Quick Ratio Quick Assets (cash, marketable securities, and receivables)/Current Liabilities				
Sales-to-Receivables (Turnover) Ratio (Net Sales/Accounts Receivable)				
Days' Receivables (365/Sales to receivables ratio)				
Cash Turnover Ratio (Net Sales/Net Working Capital)				

2. Compute the following profitability ratios for each year and draw conclusions from each ratio before making a general conclusion about profitability:

- Gross Profit Margin;

- Net Profit Margin;

- Return on Assets;

- Earnings-per-Share (EPS);

- Return on Equity Investments (Management's and Creditors' perspective); and

- Return on Investment 1 (i.e., capital appreciation).

Profitability Ratios	2019	2018	2017	2016
Gross Profit Margin (Gross Profits/Net Sales)				
Net Profit Margin (Net Income/Net Sales)				
Return on Assets (Net Income/Total Assets)				
Earnings-per-Share (EPS) Net Income/Outstanding Shares				
Return on Equity Investment Management's and Creditors' Perspective (Net Income/Owners' Equity)				
Return on Investment – Stock Investor's Perspective 1 (Stock Price Change/Previous Period's Ending Stock Price)				
Return on Investment – Stock Investor's Perspective 2 (EPS/Current Stock Price)				

3. Compute the following operating efficiency ratios for each year and draw conclusions from each ratio before making a general conclusion about operating efficiency:

- Inventory Turnover Ratio;

- Average Inventory Holding Period;

- Inventory-to-Assets Ratio;

- Accounts Receivable Turnover; and

- Average Collection Period.

Operating Efficiency Ratios	2019	2018	2017	2016
Annual inventory turnover (Cost of Goods Sold for the Year/Average Inventory)				
Inventory holding period (365/Annual Inventory Turnover)				
Inventory to assets ratio (Inventory/Total Assets)				
Accounts receivable turnover [Net (credit) Sales/Average Accounts Receivable]				
Collection period (365/Accounts Receivable Turnover)				

4. Compute the following solvency ratios for each year and draw conclusions from each ratio before making a general conclusion about solvency:

- Debt-to-Equity Ratio; and

- Debt Ratio.

5. Make a general conclusion about the financial health and performance of Vector Feeds, Inc., including its medium term prospects.

6. If Sweet Tooth, Inc. comes to you to borrow money for expanding its operations, will you or will you not lend to them? Why or why not, and use the results of your financial analysis to support your decision.

Chapter 9

Financial Statement Analysis
Case Studies Answers

<u>Vector Feeds, Inc.</u>

Liquidity Ratios	2019	2018	2017	2016	2015
Current Ratio (Current Assets/Current Liabilities)	1.54	1.12	1.28	1.35	1.11
Quick Ratio Quick Assets (cash, marketable securities, and receivables)/Current Liabilities	1.17	0.77	0.91	1.05	0.73
Sales-to-Receivables (Turnover) Ratio (Net Sales/Accounts Receivable)	11.35	11.45	12.82	13.69	13.87
Days' Receivables (365/Sales to receivables ratio)	32.16	31.86	28.46	26.67	26.31
Cash Turnover Ratio (Net Sales/Net Working Capital)	4.56	18.35	8.24	7.74	26.66

Conclusions about Liquidity:

1. Vector Feeds' current and liquidity ratios of above 1 show that they have more than enough current assets to cover their current liabilities and as such, the company's liquid.

2. However, the company's current and liquidity ratios have only recovered during the last fiscal year after two years of decline, with its quick ratios for 2017 and 2018 falling to below 1, which is the minimum expected of businesses. Until Vector Feeds' current and liquidity ratios show three straight fiscal years of either staying relatively the same or increasing, the risk of reduced liquidity is moderate.

3. The company's credit sales turnover went down from 13.87 times in 2015 to only 11.35 times as of its last fiscal year ending 2019. This has ultimately led to an increase in the average number of days' receivables from only 26.31 days during fiscal year 2015 to 32.16 days during fiscal year ending 2019. This may be red flags that the company's having an increasingly difficult time collecting from its customers. If the average number of days keeps increasing, the company's liquidity risk may increase from moderate to high.

4. Its cash turnover ratio is also something to look out for, as it dropped from 26.66 times during fiscal year 2015 to only 4.56 times during fiscal year 2019. This may be an

indication of decreased reliance on borrowings to fund operations.

5. Given conclusions 1 to 5, Vector Feeds is a liquidity company and liquidity risk is moderate.

Profitability Ratios	2019	2018	2017	2016	2015
Gross Profit Margin (Gross Profits/Net Sales)	37.82%	38.34%	38.47%	39.08%	40.06%
Net Profit Margin (Net Income/Net Sales)	21.24%	22.41%	21.09%	21.19%	22.85%
Return on Assets (Net Income/Total Assets)	16.32%	16.28%	12.88%	14.20%	18.39%
Earnings-per-Share (EPS) Net Income/Outstanding Shares	$ 0.34	$ 0.34	$ 0.26	$ 0.24	$ 0.27
Return on Equity Investment Management's and Creditors' Perspective (Net Income/Owners' Equity)	47.69%	51.38%	41.73%	39.43%	46.09%
Return on Investment – Stock Investor's Perspective 1 (Stock Price Change/Previous Period's Ending Stock Price)	15.43%	31.43%	51.51%	-2.95%	n/a
Return on Investment – Stock Investor's Perspective 2 (EPS/Current Stock Price)	5.57%	7.35%	8.59%	7.51%	n/a

Conclusions about Profitability:

1. The company's gross profits margin has declined from 40.06% in 2015 to only 37.82% in 2019, but is still high. Its net profit margin, though declined from 22.85% in 2015 to only 21.24% in 2019, is still high. These indicate the company still makes more than what it spends and is therefore, continues to be profitable. Its risk for declining profitability, however, remains high.

2. Its return on assets ratio went down from 18.39% in 2015 to only 16.32% during 2019. This indicates that the company's ability to make money off its assets has – and continues to – drop. Therefore, the risk of declining ROI ratio is very high.

3. From a management and/or creditor's perspective, the company's profitability increased according to a slightly higher return on stockholders' equity ratio of 47.69% during 2019 from 46.09% in 2015. The increase, however, was a mainly a result of a decrease in total shareholder equity due to declaration of dividends rather than an increase in revenues or decrease in expenses.

4. From the investors' perspective, the stock price of Vector Feeds, Inc. continues to rise, albeit at a slowing pace, which also slows down its return on investment through capital appreciation. From 2017's 51.51% capital appreciation, its stock price upward move has slowed down for two straight fiscal years to only 15.43% during its last fiscal year 2019,

which is still good compared to most other non-stock investments. However, this means that the chances of further slowdown in its capital appreciation are high.

5. The same goes for its return on investment, using earnings-per-share as benchmark for returns. Its ROI based on EPS and previous year's stock price has also slowed down since 2017 from 7.51% to only 5.57% in fiscal year 2019. This has been due to a slower increase in EPS compared to a higher one for its stock price.

6. Speaking of EPS, it has continued to grow over the three years from only $0.12 per share in 2016 to $0.17 for fiscal year 2019. However, the substantial increase was mainly due to the substantial reduction in outstanding number of shares in the market and less about increase in income.

7. Overall, Vector Feeds, Inc. continues to be a very profitable company and its risk of losing money is low in the near to medium term. However, profitability indicators show a declining trend in profitability, which if not addressed, may severely impact the company's viability over the long term.

Operating Efficiency Ratios	2019	2018	2017	2016	2015
Annual inventory turnover (Cost of Goods Sold for the Year/Average Inventory)	40.13	37.17	40.37	58.64	59.64
Inventory holding period (365/Annual Inventory Turnover)	9.09	9.82	9.04	6.22	6.12

Inventory to assets ratio (Inventory/Total Assets)	1.21%	1.08%	1.29%	0.66%	0.81%
Accounts receivable turnover [Net (credit) Sales/Average Accounts Receivable]	4.77	7.31	7.73	5.52	7.12
Collection period (365/Accounts Receivable Turnover)	76.50	49.96	47.21	66.11	51.25

Conclusions about Operating Efficiency:

1. The company's sales are slowing down in terms of inventory turnover and average holding periods. From 2015, its annual inventory turnover went down from 59.64 times to only 40.13 times in fiscal year 2019. This also translated to a longer average inventory holding period from 6.12 days in fiscal year 2015 to 9.09 days in fiscal year 2019. This is an indication that the company is having a harder time selling its feeds, probably due to competition from newer and more aggressive Chinese feed manufacturing firms eager to grab market share quickly.

2. As a result of a slowdown in movement of inventory, inventory has taken a greater portion of total assets than before, i.e., inventory-to-assets-ratio. From a low of 0.66% of total assets in 2016, inventory's share of total assets has grown to 1.21% of total in fiscal year 2019, albeit it's still a tiny portion of total assets.

3. Similar to inventory turnover, the company is taking longer to collect on its credit sales. This can be seen in its accounts receivables turnover and average collection period ratios. Accounts receivables turnover went down from 7.12 times in 2015 to only 4.77 times as of end of fiscal year 2019 while average collection period extended from only 51.25 days in 2015 to 76.50 days in 2019. This may be a strategic move to retain and win more customers in light of competition from new and aggressive Chinese feed-manufacturing companies.

4. Overall, Vector Feeds' operates efficiently but operational efficiency has declined in the last four years. As a result of increased competition, the risk of declining operational efficiency in the near term is high, albeit the decline isn't expected to be significant.

Solvency Ratios	2019	2018	2017	2016	2015
Debt to equity ratio (Debt/Owners' Equity)	274.10%	241.33%	179.99%	150.83%	143.26%
Debt ratio (Debt/Total Assets)	0.73	0.71	0.64	0.60	0.59

Conclusions about Solvency:

1. Based on both ratios and its shareholders' equity balances, the company remains solvent and its risk for insolvency is low as of the moment.

Overall Conclusion: Vector Foods, Inc.

Vector Foods, Inc. is in good financial condition and continues to operate profitably and efficiently. It's liquid (has more than enough liquid assets to pay for its current obligations), it's profitable, efficient, and solvent. However, risk of minor declines in financial condition and performance are moderate, given the successive declines in key indicators.

Creditors can lend to Vector Foods because it has shown that it's liquid and profitable. As an investor, investing in the company's stocks will most likely be profitable.

Genius Learning Institute, Inc.

Liquidity Ratios	2019	2018	2017	2016	2015
Current Ratio (Current Assets/Current Liabilities)	1.54	1.12	1.28	1.35	1.11
Quick Ratio Quick Assets (cash, marketable securities, and receivables)/Current Liabilities	1.17	0.77	0.91	1.05	0.73
Sales-to-Receivables (Turnover) Ratio (Net Sales/Accounts Receivable)	11.35	11.45	12.82	13.69	13.87
Days' Receivables (365/Sales to receivables ratio)	32.16	31.86	28.46	26.67	26.31
Cash Turnover Ratio (Net Sales/Net Working Capital)	4.56	18.35	8.24	7.74	26.66

Conclusions about Liquidity:

1. Genius Learning Institute, Inc.'s (GLII) current and quick ratios have improved since 2015 and being above 1.0, both ratios indicate that the company has more than enough current assets to pay for current liabilities. However, current ratio needs improvement as the ideal ratio is 2.0, to give enough leeway in case of significant and unexpected needs for cash.

2. The company's sales to receivables ratio has declined from 13.87 times in 2015 to 11.35 times in 2019, which indicates a slowdown in collection on credit sales. This is a very important factor affecting a business' liquidity.

3. The slower collection on credit sales also reflects in GLII's increasing average day's receivables collection period. From an average of 26.31 days in 2015, collection period went up to 32.16 days in 2019. This collection period extension may be an intentional strategy to manage increased competition from online courses and DIY YouTube videos, with a record number of new and much cheaper ones popping up in the market almost every week!

4. The decrease in the company's cash turnover ratio from 26.66 times in 2015 to only 4.56 times in 2019 suggests that the company has been relying less on borrowings for its operating capital, which lowers their liquidity risks, too.

5. Given the company's liquidity indicators, the GLII is a liquid company and its liquidity risk is low to moderate only.

Profitability Ratios	2019	2018	2017	2016	2015
Net Profit Margin (Net Income/Net Sales)	21.24%	22.41%	21.09%	21.19%	22.85%
Return on Assets (Net Income/Total Assets)	16.32%	16.28%	12.88%	14.20%	18.39%
Earnings-per-Share (EPS) Net Income/Outstanding Shares	$ 0.17	$ 0.17	$ 0.13	$ 0.12	$ 0.13
Return on Equity Investment Management's and Creditors' Perspective (Net Income/Owners' Equity)	47.69%	51.38%	41.73%	39.43%	46.09%
Return on Investment – Stock Investor's Perspective 1 (Stock Price Change/Previous Period's Ending Stock Price)	15.43%	31.43%	51.51%	-2.95%	n/a
Return on Investment – Stock Investor's Perspective 2 (EPS/Current Stock Price)	5.57%	7.35%	8.59%	7.51%	n/a

Conclusions about Profitability:

1. The company's net profit margin has declined since 2015, because percentage growth in sales was slower than those of operating expenses.

2. Overall, its assets' ability to produce income has also gone down, with its return on assets ratio going down from 18.39% in 2015 to only 16.32% in 2019. The risk of further decline in this ratio is moderate given the successive number of years of decline in this ratio.

3. The company's earnings per share has gone up from 2015's $0.13 to $0.17 in 2019. However, the increase was mainly due to a significant reduction in number of shares outstanding over the last four years and less due to increases in net income.

4. The company's return on equity investment has also increased, albeit slightly, since 2015 from 46.09% to 47.69% in 2019. This is primarily due to a substantial reduction in retained earnings over the last few years resulting from dividend payments to shareholders.

5. Capital appreciation, e.g., Return on Investments from investors' perspective 1, has declined since 2017 from 51.5% to 15.43% in 2019.

6. EPS as a percentage of purchase price, i.e., ROI investors' perspective 2, has improved, from only $0.13 per share in 2015 to $0.17 per share in 2019. Though net income grew over the years, primary reason for the EPS growth was a significant reduction in number of shares outstanding.

7. Overall, the company continues to operate profitably and its risk for operating losses are very low.

Operating Efficiency Ratios	2019	2018	2017	2016	2015
Accounts receivable turnover [Net (credit) Sales/Average Accounts Receivable]	4.77	7.31	7.73	5.52	7.12
Collection period (365/Accounts Receivable Turnover)	76.50	49.96	47.21	66.11	51.25

Conclusions about Operating Efficiency:

1. The company is a service provider and hence, no inventory-related ratios.

2. The company's receivables collection efficiency has gone down significantly from 2015, judging from the receivables turnover ratio and its average collection period. From 2015's 7.12 times, receivables turnover fell to only 4.77 times in 2019.

3. The speed at which the company collects on its receivables has slowed down. Its average collection period increased to 76.50 days in 2019 from only 51.25 in 2015. The intense competition from e-courses and other learning institutions may be a reason why the company seems to have intentionally extended its credit payment terms.

4. From a collection standpoint, the company remains efficient but pressure from online competitors put it at risk for further decline in operational efficiency, i.e., collecting efficiency.

Solvency Ratios	2019	2018	2017	2016	2015
Debt to equity ratio (Debt/Owners' Equity)	274.10%	241.33%	179.99%	150.83%	143.26%
Debt ratio (Debt/Total Assets)	0.73	0.71	0.64	0.60	0.59

Conclusions about Solvency:

1. Based on the company's positive shareholder equity ratio balances, the company remains solvent and the risk for insolvency in the near to medium term is low given its liquidity, profitability, and efficiency.

Overall Conclusion: Genius Learning Institute, Inc.

The company is in good financial condition and its risk for financial failure are low considering its good liquidity position, profitability, solvency, and operating efficiency. However, continuous declines in financial indicators increase its risk for further, albeit minor, declines in liquidity and operational efficiency.

With its relatively good liquidity and profitability, lending to Genius Learning Institute can be a profitable and moderate risk investment. For those looking to invest in its shares of stocks, it may be better to look for other stocks of growth companies, considering the major threat online courses pose to the company's bottom line, which may limit the potential returns on investments on its stocks.

Sweet Tooth, Inc.

Liquidity Ratios	2019	2018	2017	2016	2015
Current Ratio (Current Assets/Current Liabilities)	1.54	1.12	1.28	1.35	1.11
Quick Ratio Quick Assets (cash, marketable securities, and receivables)/Current Liabilities	1.17	0.77	0.91	1.05	0.73
Sales-to-Receivables (Turnover) Ratio (Net Sales/Accounts Receivable)	11.35	11.45	12.82	13.69	13.87
Days' Receivables (365/Sales to receivables ratio)	32.16	31.86	28.46	26.67	26.31
Cash Turnover Ratio (Net Sales/Net Working Capital)	4.56	18.35	8.24	7.74	26.66

Conclusions about Liquidity:

1. Sweet Tooth's' current and liquidity ratios of above 1 show that they have more than enough current assets to cover their current liabilities and as such, the company's liquid.

2. The company's current and quick ratios are at their 5-year highs after 2 years of slight declines. However, its current ratio has room for improvement considering it's still below the generally acceptable level of at least 2.0. Fortunately, its quick ratio is above the 1.0 minimum and thus, ensuring its quick ability to meet current financial obligations.

3. The company's sales-to-receivables turnover slowed down, indicating either a potential slowdown in collection of

receivables or an intentional extension of credit terms to maintain or increase market share amidst stiff competition.

4. Cash turnover ratio went down as well. While this is good for liquidity, meaning it's becoming less reliant on borrowings to fund inventories, too much liquidity can also make the company less profitable.

5. STI is a liquid company and liquidity risk is moderate. Creditors can lend to this company.

Profitability Ratios	2019	2018	2017	2016	2015
Gross Profit Margin (Gross Profits/Net Sales)	37.82%	38.34%	38.47%	39.08%	40.06%
Net Profit Margin (Net Income/Net Sales)	21.24%	22.41%	21.09%	21.19%	22.85%
Return on Assets (Net Income/Total Assets)	16.32%	16.28%	12.88%	14.20%	18.39%
Earnings-per-Share (EPS) Net Income/Outstanding Shares	$ 0.34	$ 0.34	$ 0.26	$ 0.24	$ 0.27
Return on Equity Investment Management's and Creditors' Perspective (Net Income/Owners' Equity)	47.69%	51.38%	41.73%	39.43%	46.09%
Return on Investment – Stock Investor's Perspective 1 (Stock	15.43%	31.43%	51.51%	-2.95%	n/a

Price Change/Previous Period's Ending Stock Price)					
Return on Investment – Stock Investor's Perspective 2 (EPS/Current Stock Price)	5.57%	7.35%	8.59%	7.51%	n/a

Conclusions about Profitability:

1. Despite the decrease in its gross profit and net profit margins, the company continues to be very profitable, with high ratios. The continuous decline in these ratios, however, may indicate a high risk of further minor declines in gross and net profit margins.

2. The company's asset profitability went down in the last five years as well, with return on assets ratios going down to 16.32% in 2019. While still highly profitable, ROA is still expected to go down given the last few years of decline.

3. Return on equity investments continues to go up over the last five years. However, this isn't completely due to the significant increase in net income. It was also due to the substantial decrease in its retained earnings in the last two years.

4. From a stock investor's perspective, the return on the stock based on capital appreciation is still good at 15.43% for

2019, though it's much slower compared to the two years prior. Nevertheless, it's much higher compared to most other types of investments outside of the stock market and its stock price is still expected to go up in the next few years given its profitable track record and international market share...

5. Return on investment based on EPS as a percentage of previous market price has also slowed down to "only" 64.99% in 2019, which is still a very high return on investment, regardless. The significantly high growth in EPS coupled with a plateauing price growth made the ROI high.

6. Speaking of EPS, it has continued to grow over the three years from only $3.09 per share in 2015 to $3.99 for fiscal year 2019. However, the substantial increase was caused largely by the great reduction in outstanding number of shares in the last three years.

7. Overall, Sweet Tooth, Inc. continues to be a very profitable company and its risk of losing money is low in the near to medium term. However, profitability indicators show a declining trend in profitability, which if not addressed, may severely impact the company's viability over the long term.

Operating Efficiency Ratios	2019	2018	2017	2016	2015
Annual inventory turnover (Cost of Goods Sold for the Year/Average Inventory)	40.13	37.17	40.37	58.64	59.64
Inventory holding period (365/Annual Inventory Turnover)	9.09	9.82	9.04	6.22	6.12
Inventory to assets ratio (Inventory/Total Assets)	1.21%	1.08%	1.29%	0.66%	0.81%
Accounts receivable turnover [Net (credit) Sales/Average Accounts Receivable]	4.77	7.31	7.73	5.52	7.12
Collection period (365/Accounts Receivable Turnover)	76.50	49.96	47.21	66.11	51.25

Conclusions about Operating Efficiency:

1. Sweet Tooth's inventory ratios both showed signs of slowing down. The longer inventory holding period (from 6.12 to 9.09 days) lead to fewer turnovers during the year (from 59.64 times to 40.13 times). This may indicate increasing difficulty in moving inventory, i.e., selling.

2. On the collections part, the company's receivables collection-related ratios also showed signs of slowing down over the last few years. Average collection period protracted from only 51 days in 2015 to almost 77 days in 2019. This may either be a sign of their customers' declining liquidity or a strategic move to maintain or increase market share in the midst of intense competition in the international sweets' market.

3. Overall, Sweet Tooth operates efficiently but has been declining lately. Being in a relatively saturated market increases its risk of further declines in operating efficiency.

Solvency Ratios	2019	2018	2017	2016	2015
Debt to equity ratio (Debt/ Owners' Equity)	274.10%	241.33%	179.99%	150.83%	143.26%
Debt ratio (Debt/Total Assets)	0.73	0.71	0.64	0.60	0.59

Conclusions about Solvency:

1. Based on both ratios and its shareholders' equity balances, the company remains solvent and its risk for insolvency is low as of the moment.

Overall Conclusion: Sweet Tooth, Inc.

Sweet Tooth, Inc. is a financially stable and profitable company. It has enough liquidity to pay off its creditors, and is thus, a worthy borrower to lend to. It continues to be very profitable, solvent, and operationally efficient. However, continuous declines in key areas, albeit minor ones only, put it at risk of further declines in those key areas. But overall, it's still a very good investment.

Chapter 10

Cost of Capital

This term refers to the minimum rate of return for proposed capital budgeting projects. These projects include new factories or capital equipment, among others. The cost of capital tells management whether it's worth undergoing a certain project or if that project needs to be rejected.

The cost of capital, in layman's terms, is how much a company pays for the money it uses to finance itself. There are two sources of financing for businesses, if you remember: capital and debt. Therefore, the cost of capital is the weighted average of the costs of debt and shareholders' equity. If the business is funded purely by equity capital, then the cost of equity is the cost of capital. If purely by debt, then average cost of all of the business' debts is the cost of capital.

There are two main users of the cost of capital concept: investors and management. Investors can use the cost of capital to determine if an investment option is worth the risk. Management of companies use the cost of capital to determine if undergoing a specific proposed project is worth it or not.

Most companies use both capital and debt to put up and run their businesses. As such, the cost of capital is the weighted average of the costs of the two. And what is weighted average?

A simple average is a method of averaging a set of numbers by giving equal weights or portions for each number in the set. That's why simple averages involve dividing the total of the values in the set by the number of items in the set.

For example, take the numbers 5, 10, 20, and 5, the sum of all being 40. To get the average of these four numbers, simply divide 40 by 4, i.e., 10. Simply dividing 40 by the number of items in the set means each of those numbers have an equal weight or contribution to the average.

Weighted averages, on the other hand, assign different weights or portions to each number of the set. The total of the weights or portions assigned to the items in the set should total 1 or 100% - no more, no less.

Let's say that the number set 5, 10, 20, and 5 is weighted such that the last number has the heaviest weight while the first has the least weight, i.e.

- 5 = 15%

- 10 = 20%;

- 20 = 30%; and

- 5 = 35%.

Computing for the weighted average, the formula is: Weighted Average $= \sum\sum I_n W_n$ where:

- n = Number in the set, i.e., sequence number or position;

- I = Value of the item in sequence n; and

- W = Weight of the item in sequence n.

Applying it to the number sequence above:

Weighted Average = 5(0.15) + 10(0.20) + 20(0.30) + 5(0.35)

Weighted Average = 0.75 + 2.00 + 6.00 + 1.75

Weighted Average = 9.75

Notice that the weighted average of the same number sequence is different from its simple average of 10. This is because of the way the numbers were weighted, which in our example placed the most weight on the last number, which was also the lowest. If more weight is given to the higher numbers, the weighted average would've been higher than the simple one.

Computing for Cost of Debt

The real cost of borrowing money is the interest expense paid on it. To find the cost of borrowing for a company is simple:

Cost of Debt = [Interest Expense ÷ Average Total Liabilities] X [1 – Tax Rate]

Interest expense, like any other legitimate business expense, is tax-deductible. Hence the cost of debt, for purposes of computing for cost of capital, is net of the tax rate, i.e., [1 – Tax Rate].

If the company's total interest expense for fiscal year 2019 was $200 thousand, its average annual total liabilities is $5 million, and its tax rate is 15%, then its cost of debt is:

Cost of Debt = [$200 thousand ÷ $5.00 million] X [1 – 15%]

Cost of Debt = 4.00% X 85%

Cost of Debt = 3.40%

Computing for Cost of Stockholders' Equity

Unlike with debt, the interest rate and/or expenses of which are clear to the company, the minimum required rate of return for shareholders' equity isn't that easy or simple. For example, some shareholders are happy with a 10% average annual rate of return on investments while others are only happy with a 15% annual rate of return.

So, how do companies' management teams estimate the cost of their shareholders' equity? One of the most popular ways of estimating cost of equity is the capital asset pricing model or CAPM, the formula of which is as follows:

Cost of Equity = Risk-Free Rate + [Beta X (Rate of Market Return – Risk-Free Rate)]

Beta is a risk measure that tells us the volatility of a company's stock price in relation to that of the markets. If a company's beta is less than 1.0, it means its price movements are less than that of the market's and hence, less risky. If the company's beta is higher than 1.0, it means that the movements in a company's stock price vis-a-vis that of the stock market's is greater and hence, riskier.

The risk-free rate, on the other hand, is the average rate of return on Federal Government-backed securities like Treasury Bills and Bonds. Why are they risk-free? They will never be in default because worst comes to worst, the United States' Federal Government can always print new dollars to pay for their debts. Hence, they're credit-risk free.

Let's say that the following are true for Vector Feeds, Inc.:

1. The average annual rate of return on the stock market is 15%;

2. The Risk-Free Rate is 4%; and

3. Beta for Vector Feeds' stock is 0.30.

Vector Feeds' cost of stockholder equity is:

Cost of Equity = Risk-Free Rate + [Beta X (Rate of Market Return – Risk-Free Rate)]

Cost of Equity = 4.00% + [0.30 X (15.00% – 4.00%)]

Cost of Equity = 4.00% + [0.30 X (11.00%)]

Cost of Equity = 4.00% + 3.30%

Cost of Equity = 7.30%

Computing for the Weighted Average Cost of Capital (WACC)

One final concept we need to cover before being able to compute for a company's weighted average cost of capital (WACC) is capital structure. This refers to the composition of the funds that support the company, i.e., how much of the company is funded by debts and how much by the owners' capital.

Remember the concept of weighted average, i.e., each of the components of an average are given different weights or portions? The capital structure of a company will tell us how much weight we'll give to the cost of debt and the cost of owners' equity.

If Vector Feeds, Inc.'s capital structure is 70% debt and 30% equity, the cost of debt will have a weight of 70% and cost of equity will have a weight of 30%.

Here's how to compute Vector Feeds' WACC:

WACC (Vector Feeds) = [70% X Cost of Debt] + [30% X Cost of Equity]

WACC (Vector Feeds) = [70% X 3.40%] + [30% X 7.30%]

WACC (Vector Feeds) = 2.38% + 2.19%

WACC (Vector Feeds) = 4.57%

Thus, the weighted average cost of capital of Vector Feeds, Inc. is 4.57% and for any projects or investments to be approved by management, their estimated rates of return must exceed 4.57%.

Discount Rate vs. Cost of Capital

These two rates are often interchanged because of the way companies use them to decide which projects to approve and disapprove. However, there is a slight difference between the two, which depends on the goal.

The cost of capital is often used as a benchmark by which to approve or disapprove a proposed project or investment. As in our example earlier, the 4.57% WACC is the hurdle that expected returns or discount rates of cash flows of proposed investments and projects must exceed to get management's "yes" answer.

However, the cost of capital can also be used as a discount rate by which to compare the present values of expected cash inflows from proposed investments or projects. If the present value is less than the initial cost of investment, then the project or investment's a go. Otherwise, it's a no.

You'll get the chance to understand in greater detail when you solve the practice cases later on.

Using WACC as Hurdle Rate for Proposed Projects/Investments

Given the following figures for Genius Learning Institute (GLII), determine whether the company must proceed with funding a new learning center for geniuses in Chicago City:

1. Cost of investment is $5 million;
2. Expected average annual rate of return of 10%;

3. Interest expenses of $700,000 for the current fiscal year;

4. Average total liabilities/debts of $10,000,000 for the current fiscal year;

5. Tax rate of 12%;

6. Risk-free rate of 3%;

7. Average annual rate of returns on stock market investments of 16%;

8. Genius Learning Institute, Inc.'s beta is 1.35; and

9. Capital structure is 45% debt and 55% equity.

Here are the steps to determine whether or not to accept the proposed new learning center in Chicago city.

Compute for Estimated Cost of Debt

Cost of Debt = [Interest Expense ÷ Average Total Liabilities] X [1 – Tax Rate]

Cost of Debt = [$700,000 ÷ $10,000,000] X [1 – 12%]

Cost of Debt = 7.00% X 88%

Cost of Debt = 6.16%

Compute for Cost of Equity

Cost of Equity = Risk-Free Rate + [Beta X (Rate of Market Return – Risk-Free Rate)]

Cost of Equity = 3.00% + [1.35 X (16.00% – 3.00%)]

Cost of Equity = 3.00% + [1.35 X (13.00%)]

Cost of Equity = 3.00% + 17.55%

Cost of Equity = 20.55%

Compute for the Weighted Average Cost of Capital

WACC (GLII) = [45% X Cost of Debt] + [55% X Cost of Equity]

WACC (GLII) = [45% X 6.16%] + [55% X 20.55%]

WACC (GLII) = 2.77% + 11.30%

WACC (GLII) = 14.07%

Make the Decision

Considering that the company's WACC is 14.07%, which is higher than the proposed new learning center in Chicago's estimated average annual rate of return of only 10%, the company should reject the proposed new learning center.

Chapter 11

Exercises for Cost of Capital and Investments

Exercise #1: Forefoot Running Gear, Inc. (FRGI)

Given the following figures for Forefoot Running Gear, Inc. (FRGI), determine whether the company must proceed with building a new plant in Vietnam:

1. Expected average annual rate of return of 17%;

2. Interest expenses of $900,000 for the current fiscal year;

3. Average total liabilities/debts of $13,000,000 for the current fiscal year;

4. Tax rate of 17%;

5. Risk-free rate of 4%;

6. Average annual rate of returns on stock market investments of 13%;

7. Forefoot Running Gear, Inc.'s beta is 0.87; and

8. Capital structure is 30% debt and 70% equity.

Here are the steps to determine whether or not to approve the construction of the proposed plant in Vietnam:

Compute for Estimated Cost of Debt

Cost of Debt = [Interest Expense ÷ Average Total Liabilities] X [1 – Tax Rate]

Cost of Debt = [$900,000 ÷ $13,000,000] X [1 – 17%]

Cost of Debt = 6.92% X 83%

Cost of Debt = 5.75%

Compute for Cost of Equity

Cost of Equity = Risk-Free Rate + [Beta X (Rate of Market Return – Risk-Free Rate)]

Cost of Equity = 4.00% + [0.87 X (13.00% – 4.00%)]

Cost of Equity = 4.00% + [0.87 X (9.00%)]

Cost of Equity = 4.00% + 7.83%

Cost of Equity = 11.83%

Compute for the Weighted Average Cost of Capital

WACC (FRGI) = [30% X Cost of Debt] + [70% X Cost of Equity]

WACC (FRGI) = [30% X 5.75%] + [70% X 11.83%]

WACC (FRGI) = 1.72% + 8.28%

WACC (FRGI) = 10.00%

Make the Decision

Considering that the company's WACC is only 10.07%, which is lower than the proposed new plant's estimated average annual rate of return of 17.00%, the company should approve the proposed new plant in Vietnam.

Exercise #2: All American Burgers, Inc. (AABI)

Given the following figures for All American Burgers, Inc. (AABI), determine whether the company must proceed with opening a new branch in Minnesota:

1. Expected average annual rate of return of 13.00%;

2. Interest expenses of $1,300,000 for the current fiscal year;

3. Average total liabilities/debts of $20,000,000 for the current fiscal year;

4. Tax rate of 19%;

5. Risk-free rate of 2%;

6. Average annual rate of returns on stock market investments of 14%;

7. All American Burger, Inc.'s beta is 1.25; and

8. Capital structure is 55% debt and 45% equity.

Here are the steps to determine whether or not to approve the opening of a new branch in Minnesota:

Compute for Estimated Cost of Debt

Cost of Debt = [Interest Expense ÷ Average Total Liabilities] X [1 – Tax Rate]

Cost of Debt = [$1,300,000 ÷ $20,000,000] X [1 – 19%]

Cost of Debt = 6.50% X 81.00%

Cost of Debt = 5.27%

Compute for Cost of Equity

Cost of Equity = Risk-Free Rate + [Beta X (Rate of Market Return – Risk-Free Rate)]

Cost of Equity = 2.00% + [1.25 X (14.00% – 2.00%)]

Cost of Equity = 2.00% + [1.25 X (12.00%)]

Cost of Equity = 2.00% + 15.00%

Cost of Equity = 17.00%

Compute for the Weighted Average Cost of Capital

WACC (AABI) = [55% X Cost of Debt] + [45% X Cost of Equity]

WACC (AABI) = [55% X 5.27%] + [45% X 17.00%]

WACC (AABI) = 2.90% + 7.65%

WACC (AABI) = 10.55%

Make the Decision

Considering that the company's WACC is only 10.55%, which is lower than the proposed new plant's estimated average annual rate of return of 13.00%, the company should approve the proposed new branch in Minnesota.

Exercise #3: Computer Chips Power, Inc. (CCP)

Given the following figures for Computer Chips Power, Inc. (CCP), determine whether the company must proceed with investing in one of its most important supplier companies in China:

1. Expected average annual rate of return of 13%;

2. Interest expenses of $500,000 for the current fiscal year;

3. Average total liabilities/debts of $3,000,000 for the current fiscal year;

4. Tax rate of 20%;

5. Risk-free rate of 2%;

6. Average annual rate of returns on stock market investments of 15%;

7. Computer Chips Power, Inc.'s beta is 1.50; and

8. Capital structure is 70% debt and 30% equity.

Here are the steps to determine whether or not to approve the proposed investment in one of its most important supplier companies:

Compute for Estimated Cost of Debt

Cost of Debt = [Interest Expense ÷ Average Total Liabilities] X [1 – Tax Rate]

Cost of Debt = [$500,000 ÷ $3,000,000] X [1 – 20%]

Cost of Debt = 16.67% X 80%

Cost of Debt = 13.33%

Compute for Cost of Equity

Cost of Equity = Risk-Free Rate + [Beta X (Rate of Market Return – Risk-Free Rate)]

Cost of Equity = 2.00% + [1.50 X (15.00% – 2.00%)]

Cost of Equity = 2.00% + [1.50 X (13.00%)]

Cost of Equity = 2.00% + 19.50%

Cost of Equity = 21.50%

Compute for the Weighted Average Cost of Capital

WACC (CCP) = [70% X Cost of Debt] + [30% X Cost of Equity]

WACC (CCP) = [70% X 13.33%] + [30% X 21.50%]

WACC (CCP) = 9.33% + 6.45%

WACC (CCP) = 15.78%

Make the Decision

Considering that the company's WACC is 15.78%, which is higher than the proposed investment's estimated average annual rate of return of 13.00% only, the company should disapprove said investment in the company of one of its most important suppliers.

Exercise #4: Forever Fashion, Inc. (FFI)

Given the following figures for Forever Fashion, Inc. (FFI), determine whether the company must proceed with putting up a new fashion outlet along Rodeo Drive in L.A.:

1. Expected average annual rate of return of 20%;

2. Interest expenses of $1,300,000 for the current fiscal year;

3. Average total liabilities/debts of $11,000,000 for the current fiscal year;

4. Tax rate of 19%;

5. Risk-free rate of 1%;

6. Average annual rate of returns on stock market investments of 17%;

7. Forever Fashion, Inc.'s beta is 0.50; and

8. Capital structure is 50% debt and 50% equity.

Here are the steps to determine whether or not to approve the proposed opening of a new fashion outlet in L.A.:

Compute for Estimated Cost of Debt

Cost of Debt = [Interest Expense ÷ Average Total Liabilities] X [1 – Tax Rate]

Cost of Debt = [$1,300,000 ÷ $11,000,000] X [1 – 19%]

Cost of Debt = 11.82% X 81%

Cost of Debt = 9.57%

Compute for Cost of Equity

Cost of Equity = Risk-Free Rate + [Beta X (Rate of Market Return – Risk-Free Rate)]

Cost of Equity = 1.00% + [0.50 X (17.00% – 1.00%)]

Cost of Equity = 1.00% + [0.50 X (16.00%)]

Cost of Equity = 1.00% + 8.00%

Cost of Equity = 9.00%

Compute for the Weighted Average Cost of Capital

WACC (FFI) = [50% X Cost of Debt] + [50% X Cost of Equity]

WACC (FFI) = [50% X 9.57%] + [50% X 9.00%]

WACC (FFI) = 4.79% + 4.50%

WACC (FFI) = 9.29%

Make the Decision

Considering that the company's WACC is only 9.29%, which is way lower than the proposed new L.A. outlet's estimated average annual rate of return of 20.00%, the company should approve the proposed new fashion outlet along Rodeo Drive in L.A.

Exercise #5: WePay Remittance, Inc. (WPRI)

Given the following figures for WePay Remittance, Inc. (WPRI), determine whether the company must proceed with opening a new regional office in Manila, Philippines:

1. Expected average annual rate of return of 15%;

2. Interest expenses of $500,000 for the current fiscal year;

3. Average total liabilities/debts of $12,500,000 for the current fiscal year;

4. Tax rate of 10%;

5. Risk-free rate of 2%;

6. Average annual rate of returns on stock market investments of 17%;

7. WePay Remittance, Inc.'s (WPRI) beta is 1.00; and

8. Capital structure is 80% debt and 20% equity.

Here are the steps to determine whether or not to approve the proposed opening of a new regional office in Manila, Philippines:

Compute for Estimated Cost of Debt

Cost of Debt = [Interest Expense ÷ Average Total Liabilities] X [1 – Tax Rate]

Cost of Debt = [$500,000 ÷ $1,250,000] X [1 – 10%]

Cost of Debt = 4.00% X 90%

Cost of Debt = 3.60%

Compute for Cost of Equity

Cost of Equity = Risk-Free Rate + [Beta X (Rate of Market Return – Risk-Free Rate)]

Cost of Equity = 2.00% + [1.00 X (17.00% – 2.00%)]

Cost of Equity = 2.00% + [1.00 X (15.00%)]

Cost of Equity = 2.00% + 15.00%

Cost of Equity = 17.00%

Compute for the Weighted Average Cost of Capital

WACC (WPRI) = [80% X Cost of Debt] + [20% X Cost of Equity]

WACC (WPRI) = [80% X 3.60%] + [20% X 17.00%]

WACC (WPRI) = 2.88%+ 3.40%

WACC (WPRI) = 6.28%

Make the Decision

Considering that the company's WACC is only 6.28%, which is lower than the proposed new regional office's estimated average annual rate of return of 15.00%, the company should approve the proposed new office in Manila, Philippines.

Chapter 12

Exercises for Investment Analysis Using Discounted Cash Flow Analysis and Weighted Average Cost of Capital

Exercise #1: Meathead Steak House, Inc.

Meathead Steak House, Inc. (MSHI) is a chain of steak restaurants that have been gaining popularity in the last 10 years across the United States. It is currently evaluating a proposal for putting up a new regional distribution center in Houston, Texas and the following are the details of the proposed project:

1. Estimated investment cost of $5,000,000;

2. Interest expenses of $500,000 for the current fiscal year;

3. Average total liabilities/debts of $12,500,000 for the current fiscal year;

4. Tax rate of 10%;

5. Risk-free rate of 2%;

6. Average annual rate of returns on stock market investments of 17%;

7. Meathead Steak House, Inc.'s (MSHI) beta is 1.00; and

8. Capital structure is 80% debt and 20% equity.

Here are the estimated average annual net cash inflows for the next 10 years resulting from the proposed new regional distribution center in Houston, Texas:

1. $500,000 for Year 1;

2. $550,000 for Year 2;

3. $600,000 for Year 3;

4. $590,000 for Year 4;

5. $530,000 for Year 5;

6. $540,000 for Year 6;

7. $570,000 for Year 7;

8. $580,000 for Year 8;

9. $600,000 for Year 9; and

10. $605,000 for Year 10

Here are the steps to determine whether or not to approve the proposed opening of a new regional distribution center in Houston, Texas:

Compute for the Company's Weighted Average Cost of Capital (WACC)

Compute for Estimated Cost of Debt

Cost of Debt = [Interest Expense ÷ Average Total Liabilities] X [1 – Tax Rate]

Cost of Debt = [$500,000 ÷ $1,250,000] X [1 – 10%]

Cost of Debt = 4.00% X 90%

Cost of Debt = 3.60%

Compute for Cost of Equity

Cost of Equity = Risk-Free Rate + [Beta X (Rate of Market Return – Risk-Free Rate)]

Cost of Equity = 2.00% + [1.00 X (17.00% – 2.00%)]

Cost of Equity = 2.00% + [1.00 X (15.00%)]

Cost of Equity = 2.00% + 15.00%

Cost of Equity = 17.00%

Compute for the Weighted Average Cost of Capital

WACC (MSHI) = [80% X Cost of Debt] + [20% X Cost of Equity]

WACC (MSHI) = [80% X 3.60%] + [20% X 17.00%]

WACC (MSHI) = 2.88% + 3.40%

WACC (MSHI) = 6.28%

Use the WACC as Discount Rate to Get Net Present Value (NPV) of Net Cash Inflows

Year	Expected Cash Inflow at End of Period	Discount Rate	Net Present Value
1	$ 500,000.00	6.28%	$ 470,455.40
2	$ 550,000.00	6.28%	$ 486,922.23
3	$ 600,000.00	6.28%	$ 499,800.42
4	$ 590,000.00	6.28%	$ 462,429.82
5	$ 530,000.00	6.28%	$ 390,857.22
6	$ 540,000.00	6.28%	$ 374,700.68
7	$ 570,000.00	6.28%	$ 372,146.58
8	$ 580,000.00	6.28%	$ 356,299.84
9	$ 600,000.00	6.28%	$ 346,806.59
10	$ 605,000.00	6.28%	$ 329,033.35
		Total	**$4,089,452.12**

Make the Decision

Because the NPV of all the expected future net cash inflows (using the computed WACC) of $4.09 million is less than the initial estimated project investment cost of $5.00 million, the proposed project must be rejected. Why?

When NPV – using the WACC as discount rate – is less than the initial investment cost of the project, it means that the estimated rate of return for the project will be less than its WACC, which is the hurdle rate for all proposed projects and investments.

Exercise #2: Drifters Company, Inc

Drifters Company, Inc. (DCI) is one of the fastest rising car customizing companies in the United States, with over 10 branches in 10 different states put up in its first 5 years. Recently, an opportunity to open an 11th branch in a state where DCI doesn't have a branch yet has opened up. Here are the relevant figures for this proposed new branch:

1. Estimated investment cost of $3,000,000;

2. Expected average annual rate of return of 20%;

3. Interest expenses of $1,300,000 for the current fiscal year;

4. Average total liabilities/debts of $11,000,000 for the current fiscal year;

5. Tax rate of 19%;

6. Risk-free rate of 1%;

7. Average annual rate of returns on stock market investments of 17%;

8. Drifters Company, Inc.'s beta is 0.50; and

9. Capital structure is 50% debt and 50% equity.

Here are the estimated average annual net cash inflows for the next 10 years resulting from the proposed new branch:

1. $400,000 for Year 1;

2. $370,000 for Year 2;

3. $370,000 for Year 3;

4. $390,000 for Year 4;

5. $400,000 for Year 5;

6. $420,000 for Year 6;

7. $430,000 for Year 7;

8. $450,000 for Year 8;

9. $500,000 for Year 9; and

10. $510,000 for Year 10

Here are the steps to determine whether or not to approve the proposed opening of a new branch for DCI:

Compute for the Company's Weighted Average Cost of Capital (WACC)

Compute for Estimated Cost of Debt

Cost of Debt = [Interest Expense ÷ Average Total Liabilities] X [1 – Tax Rate]

Cost of Debt = [$1,300,000 ÷ $11,000,000] X [1 – 19%]

Cost of Debt = 11.82% X 81%

Cost of Debt = 9.57%

Compute for Cost of Equity

Cost of Equity = Risk-Free Rate + [Beta X (Rate of Market Return – Risk-Free Rate)]

Cost of Equity = 1.00% + [0.50 X (17.00% – 1.00%)]

Cost of Equity = 1.00% + [0.50 X (16.00%)]

Cost of Equity = 1.00% + 8.00%

Cost of Equity = 9.00%

Compute for the Weighted Average Cost of Capital

WACC (DCI) = [50% X Cost of Debt] + [50% X Cost of Equity]

WACC (DCI) = [50% X 9.57%] + [50% X 9.00%]

WACC (DCI) = 4.79% + 4.50%

WACC (DCI) = 9.29%

Use the WACC as Discount Rate to Get Net Present Value (NPV) of Net Cash Inflows

Year	Expected Cash Inflow at End of Period	Discount Rate	Net Present Value
1	$400,000.00	9.29%	$ 365,998.72
2	$400,000.00	9.29%	$ 334,887.66
3	$450,000.00	9.29%	$ 344,723.77
4	$450,000.00	9.29%	$ 315,421.15
5	$500,000.00	9.29%	$ 320,677.05
6	$500,000.00	9.29%	$ 293,418.47
7	$550,000.00	9.29%	$ 295,324.66
8	$550,000.00	9.29%	$ 270,221.12
9	$600,000.00	9.29%	$ 269,728.86
10	$600,000.00	9.29%	$ 246,801.04
		Total	**$3,057,202.49**

<u>Make the Decision</u>

Because the NPV of all the expected future net cash inflows (using the computed WACC) of $3.06 million is higher than the initial estimated project investment cost of $3.00 million, the proposed project can be accepted. Why?

When NPV – using the WACC as discount rate – is higher than the initial investment cost of the project, it means that the estimated rate of return for the project will be higher than its WACC, which is the hurdle rate for all proposed projects and investments.

Exercise # 3: Max Fitness, Inc.

Max Fitness, Inc. (MFI) is a fast growing chain of Cross-Fit gyms across the US. In its first 5 years, it has already given birth to 7 other branches in 4 different states.

A few months ago, someone offered the company the opportunity to expand further, this time Boston, Massachusetts, the details of which are as follows:

1. Estimated investment cost of $7,000,000;

2. Expected average annual rate of return of 13%;

3. Interest expenses of $500,000 for the current fiscal year;

4. Average total liabilities/debts of $3,000,000 for the current fiscal year;

5. Tax rate of 20%;

6. Risk-free rate of 2%;

7. Average annual rate of returns on stock market investments of 15%;

8. Max Fitness, Inc.'s beta is 1.50; and

9. Capital structure is 70% debt and 30% equity.

Here are the estimated average annual net cash inflows for the next 10 years resulting from the proposed new regional distribution center in Houston, Texas:

1. $500,000 for Year 1;

2. $550,000 for Year 2;

3. $600,000 for Year 3;

4. $590,000 for Year 4;

5. $530,000 for Year 5;

6. $540,000 for Year 6;

7. $570,000 for Year 7;

8. $580,000 for Year 8;

9. $600,000 for Year 9; and

10. $605,000 for Year 10

Here are the steps to determine whether or not to approve the proposed opening of a new regional distribution center in Houston, Texas:

Compute for the Company's Weighted Average Cost of Capital (WACC)

Cost of Debt = [Interest Expense ÷ Average Total Liabilities] X [1 – Tax Rate]

Cost of Debt = [$500,000 ÷ $3,000,000] X [1 – 20%]

Cost of Debt = 16.67% X 80%

Cost of Debt = 13.33%

Compute for Cost of Equity

Cost of Equity = Risk-Free Rate + [Beta X (Rate of Market Return – Risk-Free Rate)]

Cost of Equity = 2.00% + [1.50 X (15.00% – 2.00%)]

Cost of Equity = 2.00% + [1.50 X (13.00%)]

Cost of Equity = 2.00% + 19.50%

Cost of Equity = 21.50%

Compute for the Weighted Average Cost of Capital

WACC (MFI) = [70% X Cost of Debt] + [30% X Cost of Equity]

WACC (MFI) = [70% X 13.33%] + [30% X 21.50%]

WACC (MFI) = 9.33% + 6.45%

WACC (MFI) = 15.78%

Use the WACC as Discount Rate to Get Net Present Value (NPV) of Net Cash Inflows

Year	Expected Cash Inflow at End of Period	Discount Rate	Net Present Value
1	$800,000.00	15.78%	$ 690,965.62

2	$800,000.00	15.78%	$ 596,791.87
3	$800,000.00	15.78%	$ 515,453.33
4	$800,000.00	15.78%	$ 445,200.67
5	$800,000.00	15.78%	$ 384,522.95
6	$850,000.00	15.78%	$ 352,872.37
7	$850,000.00	15.78%	$ 304,778.35
8	$850,000.00	15.78%	$ 263,239.20
9	$850,000.00	15.78%	$ 227,361.55
10	$850,000.00	15.78%	$ 196,373.77
		Total	**$3,977,559.67**

<u>Make the Decision</u>

Because the NPV of all the expected future net cash inflows (using the computed WACC) of only $3.98 million are less than the initial estimated project investment cost of $7.00 million, the proposed project must be rejected. Why?

When NPV – using the WACC as discount rate – is less than the initial investment cost of the project, it means that the estimated rate of return for the project will be less than its WACC, which is the hurdle rate for all proposed projects and investments.

Exercise # 4: Aqua Haven Resorts, Inc.

Aqua Haven Resorts, Inc. (AHRI) is a 15-year old resort that is considering expanding by opening a new beach resort in the

Philippine Island of Palawan. The following are the details of the project and the company itself:

1. Estimated investment cost of $10,000,000;

2. Expected average annual rate of return of 13.00%;

3. Interest expenses of $1,300,000 for the current fiscal year;

4. Average total liabilities/debts of $20,000,000 for the current fiscal year;

5. Tax rate of 19%;

6. Risk-free rate of 2%;

7. Average annual rate of returns on stock market investments of 14%;

8. Aqua Haven Resorts, Inc.'s beta is 1.25; and

9. Capital structure is 55% debt and 45% equity.

Here are the estimated average annual net cash inflows for the next 10 years resulting from the proposed new regional distribution center in Houston, Texas:

1. $1,000,000 for Year 1;

2. $1,200,000 for Year 2;

3. $1,500,000 for Year 3;

4. $1,700,000 for Year 4;

5. $1,700,000 for Year 5;

6. $2,000,000 for Year 6;

7. $2,000,000 for Year 7;

8. $2,500,000 for Year 8;

9. $2,500,000 for Year 9; and

10. $3,000,000 for Year 10

Here are the steps to determine whether or not to approve the opening of a new beach resort in Palawan, Philippines:

Compute for Estimated Cost of Debt

Cost of Debt = [Interest Expense ÷ Average Total Liabilities] X [1 – Tax Rate]

Cost of Debt = [$1,300,000 ÷ $20,000,000] X [1 – 19%]

Cost of Debt = 6.50% X 81.00%

Cost of Debt = 5.27%

Compute for Cost of Equity

Cost of Equity = Risk-Free Rate + [Beta X (Rate of Market Return – Risk-Free Rate)]

Cost of Equity = 2.00% + [1.25 X (14.00% – 2.00%)]

Cost of Equity = 2.00% + [1.25 X (12.00%)]

Cost of Equity = 2.00% + 15.00%

Cost of Equity = 17.00%

Compute for the Weighted Average Cost of Capital

WACC (AHRI) = [55% X Cost of Debt] + [45% X Cost of Equity]

WACC (AHRI) = [55% X 5.27%] + [45% X 17.00%]

WACC (AHRI) = 2.90% + 7.65%

WACC (AHRI) = 10.55%

Use the WACC as Discount Rate to Get Net Present Value (NPV) of Net Cash Inflows

Year	Expected Cash Inflow at End of Period	Discount Rate	Net Present Value
1	$ 1,000,000.00	10.55%	$ 904,568.07
2	$1,200,000.00	10.55%	$ 981,892.07
3	$ 1,500,000.00	10.55%	$ 1,110,235.27
4	$1,700,000.00	10.55%	$ 1,138,187.82
5	$1,700,000.00	10.55%	$1,029,568.36
6	$2,000,000.00	10.55%	$ 1,095,664.31
7	$2,000,000.00	10.55%	$ 991,102.95
8	$2,500,000.00	10.55%	$ 1,120,650.10
9	$2,500,000.00	10.55%	$ 1,013,704.29
10	$3,000,000.00	10.55%	$1,100,357.44
		Total	**$10,485,930.67**

Make the Decision

Because the NPV of all the expected future net cash inflows (using the computed WACC) is higher than the initial estimated project investment cost of $10.00 million, the proposed project can be accepted. Why?

When NPV – using the WACC as discount rate – is greater than the initial investment cost of the project, it means that the estimated rate of return for the project will be greater than its WACC, which is the hurdle rate for all proposed projects and investments.

Exercise # 5: Life Savers, Inc.

Life Savers, Inc. (LSI) is a 50-year old chain of hospitals all over the United States. They're considering opening a new hospital in Cleveland, Ohio, and here are the details of the proposed project and the company:

1. Estimated investment cost of $15,000,000;

2. Expected average annual rate of return of 17%;

3. Interest expenses of $900,000 for the current fiscal year;

4. Average total liabilities/debts of $13,000,000 for the current fiscal year;

5. Tax rate of 17%;

6. Risk-free rate of 4%;

7. Average annual rate of returns on stock market investments of 13%;

8. Life Savers, Inc.'s beta is 0.87; and

9. Capital structure is 30% debt and 70% equity.

Here are the estimated average annual net cash inflows for the next
10 years resulting from the proposed new regional distribution
center in Houston, Texas:

1. $1,500,000 for Year 1;

2. $1,500,000 for Year 2;

3. $2,000,000 for Year 3;

4. $2,000,000 for Year 4;

5. $2,500,000 for Year 5;

6. $2,500,000 for Year 6;

7. $3,000,000 for Year 7;

8. $3,000,000 for Year 8;

9. $3,500,000 for Year 9; and

10. $3,500,000 for Year 10

Here are the steps to determine whether or not to approve the
proposed opening of a new hospital in Cleveland, Ohio:

Compute for the Company's Weighted Average Cost of Capital (WACC)

Compute for Estimated Cost of Debt

Cost of Debt = [Interest Expense ÷ Average Total Liabilities] X [1 – Tax Rate]

Cost of Debt = [$900,000 ÷ $13,000,000] X [1 – 17%]

Cost of Debt = 6.92% X 83%

Cost of Debt = 5.75%

Compute for Cost of Equity

Cost of Equity = Risk-Free Rate + [Beta X (Rate of Market Return – Risk-Free Rate)]

Cost of Equity = 4.00% + [0.87 X (13.00% – 4.00%)]

Cost of Equity = 4.00% + [0.87 X (9.00%)]

Cost of Equity = 4.00% + 7.83%

Cost of Equity = 11.83%

Compute for the Weighted Average Cost of Capital

WACC (FRGI) = [30% X Cost of Debt] + [70% X Cost of Equity]

WACC (FRGI) = [30% X 5.75%] + [70% X 11.83%]

WACC (FRGI) = 1.72% + 8.28%

WACC (FRGI) = 10.00%

Use the WACC as Discount Rate to Get Net Present Value (NPV) of Net Cash Inflows

Year	Expected Cash Inflow at End of Period	Discount Rate	Net Present Value
1	$1,500,000.00	10.00%	$ 1,363,636.36
2	$1,500,000.00	10.00%	$ 1,239,669.42
3	$2,000,000.00	10.00%	$ 1,502,629.60
4	$2,000,000.00	10.00%	$ 1,366,026.91
5	$2,500,000.00	10.00%	$ 1,552,303.31
6	$2,500,000.00	10.00%	$ 1,411,184.83
7	$3,000,000.00	10.00%	$ 1,539,474.35
8	$3,000,000.00	10.00%	$ 1,399,522.14
9	$3,500,000.00	10.00%	$ 1,484,341.66
10	$3,500,000.00	10.00%	$ 1,349,401.51
		Total	**$14,208,190.10**

Make the Decision

Because the NPV of all the expected future net cash inflows (using the computed WACC) of $14.21 million is less than the initial estimated project investment cost of $15.00 million, the proposed project must be rejected. Why?

When NPV – using the WACC as discount rate – is less than the initial investment cost of the project, it means that the estimated rate of return for the project will be less than its WACC, which is the hurdle rate for all proposed projects and investments.

Chapter 13

Analyzing Investments

Companies need to continue growing in profitability and asset size. Otherwise, they run the risk of being overtaken by their competitors and ultimately, shut down. Increasing profitability and asset size over time requires making wise investments.

But what is a wise investment? For one, it's one that will provide opportunities for a company to earn significant returns on its money. In particular, it has to be significantly higher than the risk-free rate, which is the average annual rate of return on Federal Government securities like Treasury Bills and Bonds or even better, the average annual return on the stock market. Why?

If a company can earn 2% a year on its money without credit risk by investing in Federal Government securities, why should it invest in a project that will earn just 3%, which has a relatively moderate to high risk of losing money?

Or why would a company invest its money in a new line of business with a 50% chance of succeeding when it can invest in the stocks of blue chip companies, which can provide lower risk but potentially higher returns together with high liquidity? The potential return on that new business must be significantly higher than the average return on blue chip stocks to make it worth a company's while.

So, how do companies sift wise investments from foolish ones?

Expected Future Values

Given the same amount of investment, time frame, compounding frequencies, and levels of risk, the investment with the highest expected future value is the wisest choice. A higher future value given the same amount of investment means greater returns on investment.

Discounted Values, i.e., Present Values

Given the same amount of expected future values, time frame, compounding frequencies, and levels of risk, the investment with the lowest discounted or present value is the wisest choice. Why?

Given the same amount of future values, a lower present or discounted value means a bigger income or return. If you buy a no-coupon bond with a maturity value of $10,000 after 10 years for only $7,000, you'll earn $3,000 in profits at maturity. But if you buy the same for only $6,000, you'll earn a $4,000 profit at maturity.

Rates of Return

When comparing investment opportunities, it's important to compare apples to apples and kiwis with, well, kiwis! Or oranges. Or bananas, whatever.

Comparing future and present values of investments are practical and accurate but only for comparing investment opportunities with the same parameters, i.e., time frame, rate of return, and compounding/discounting frequency. But in most cases, investment opportunities have different parameters, making direct comparisons of discounted and compounded values unwise.

To ensure proper comparison of investment alternatives, it's important to compute for each investment's average annual rate of return. By doing this, you can compare an apple investment with an apple investment and an orange investment with an orange one, too.

How does it look like? Consider two investment alternatives:

	Investment A	**Investment B**
Initial Investment	$50,000.00	$55,000.00
Number of Years	3	4
Compounding Frequency	1	1
Future Value	$57,000.00	$62,000.00

Using the formula for getting the growth rate of Investment A:

Average Annual Growth Rate = $[\{\$57,000 \div \$50,000\}^{1 \div (1 \times 3)} - 1] \times 1$

Average Annual Growth Rate = $[\{1.14\}^{1 \div (3)} - 1] \times 1$

Average Annual Growth Rate = [{1.14}$^{0.33}$ – 1] X 1

Average Annual Growth Rate = [1.0446 – 1] X 1

Average Annual Growth Rate = 0.0446 X 1

Average Annual Growth Rate Investment A = 0.0446 or 4.46%

Using the formula for getting the growth rate of Investment B:

Average Annual Growth Rate = [{\$62,000 ÷ \$55,000}$^{1÷(1 \text{ X } 4)}$ – 1] X 1

Average Annual Growth Rate = [{1.1273}$^{1÷(4)}$ – 1] X 1

Average Annual Growth Rate = [{1.1273}$^{0.25}$ – 1] X 1

Average Annual Growth Rate = [1.0304 – 1] X 1

Average Annual Growth Rate = 0.0304 X 1

Average Annual Growth Rate Investment B = 0.0304 or 3.04%

While Investment B has a higher future value than Investment A, it also has a higher initial investment. Because Investment A has a lower investment cost and shorter time frame, it has a higher rate of return on investment.

Now, let us look at two investments with the same time frame but different compounding frequencies.

	Investment A	**Investment B**
Initial Investment	\$50,000.00	\$48,000.00
Number of Years	4	4
Compounding Frequency	1 (Annual)	4 (Quarterly)
Future Value	\$57,000.00	\$56,000.00

Using the formula for getting the growth rate of Investment A:

Average Annual Growth Rate = $[\{\$57,000 \div \$50,000\}^{1\div(4 \text{ X } 1)} - 1] \text{ X } 1$

Average Annual Growth Rate = $[\{1.1400\}^{1\div(4)} - 1] \text{ X } 1$

Average Annual Growth Rate = $[\{1.1400\}^{0.25} - 1] \text{ X } 1$

Average Annual Growth Rate = $[1.\ 1.0333 - 1] \text{ X } 1$

Average Annual Growth Rate = $0.0333 \text{ X } 1$

Average Annual Growth Rate Investment A = 0.0333 or 3.33%

Using the formula for getting the growth rate of Investment B:

Average Annual Growth Rate = $[\{\$56,000 \div \$48,000\}^{1\div(4 \text{ X } 4)} - 1] \text{ X } 4$

Average Annual Growth Rate = $[\{1.1667\}^{1\div(16)} - 1] \text{ X } 4$

Average Annual Growth Rate = $[\{1.1667\}^{0.0625} - 1] \text{ X } 4$

Average Annual Growth Rate = $[1.0097 - 1] \text{ X } 4$

Average Annual Growth Rate = $0.0097 \text{ X } 4$

Average Annual Growth Rate Investment B = 0.0388 or 3.88%

Despite having a smaller future value, Investment B's smaller initial investment coupled with more frequent compounding (quarterly) gave it a higher rate of return of 3.88% compared to Investment A's 3.33%. Hence, Investment B's the wiser investment choice.

Discounted Cash Flows

The examples above are quite simple to compare because they assume a single cash inflow. But what about projects that provide multiple income or cash inflows across a period of time, such as a property that's being rented or a new factory? Worse, what if each year's cash flow differs in amount? How can you compare investment or project options wisely?

The principle of discounting still applies except that, the analyst must discount each of the expected cash inflow amounts back to the present and add them all up to get the total discounted cash flows. If the total discounted cash flows are equal to or higher than the initial cost of investment, the project is a good one and should be undertaken. If less than the initial cost of investment, it should be rejected.

Why?

If the total of the discounted cash flows are lower than the proposed initial investment cost, it means you can you can get the same amount of future cash inflows at a lower investment cost. Why pay higher for the same benefits, right?

If the total of the discounted cash inflows are higher than the proposed initial investment cost, it means you have the opportunity to enjoy the same future cash inflows at a lower cost. Hence, the proposed project or investment's a go.

Here's an example to give you a clearer picture:

A manufacturing company's thinking of whether to push through with expansion by putting up a new plant in Southeast Asia. The proposed initial cost of investment is $500,000 and the new plant is expected to contribute a series of cash inflows to the company for 10 years. Further, let's say that the company's minimum required return on investments is 7% annually.

Here are the amounts of expected cash inflows from the new plant and their discounted values:

End of Year	Expected Cash Inflows	Discount Rate	Present Value of Cash Inflows
1	$ 50,000.00	7%	$ 46,728.97
2	$ 55,000.00	7%	$ 53,170.51
3	$ 55,000.00	7%	$ 53,773.47
4	$ 56,000.00	7%	$ 55,060.74
5	$ 57,000.00	7%	$ 56,233.89
6	$ 57,000.00	7%	$ 56,360.85
7	$ 56,000.00	7%	$ 55,461.34
8	$ 55,000.00	7%	$ 54,536.81
9	$ 60,000.00	7%	$ 59,550.63
10	$ 59,000.00	7%	$ 58,602.16
Total Discounted Cash Flows			**$549,479.38**

Given that the present value of all the expected future cash inflows from the proposed new plant is much greater than the proposed $500,000 initial investment, it means the company will likely earn more than 7% on its $500,000 plant investment. Hence, the project is a go.

What if the initial cost of investment for the same proposed plant was $600,000? Given that the discounted values of all the expected future cash inflows combined is less than the proposed initial cost of investment, the company will not earn a minimum of 7% return on this investment. Hence, it should not be approved.

The Price-to-Earnings (P/E) Ratio

Earlier on the section of profitability, we discussed Earnings-per-Share (EPS) and computing the return on investment on a company's share of stock vis-a-vis its market price. If you recall, the formula for that version of the ROI is:

ROI = EPS ÷ Current Stock Price

This gives investors an idea of their likely return on a company's stock if they buy from the market now and assuming current EPS will be the same. However, the same ratio can be literally turned on its head to evaluate whether a company's stock is expensive or cheap. The inversion of this ROI formula is the P/E ratio.

The P/E ratio is a number that tells you how much investors are currently willing to pay to get the chance to earn a stock's EPS. A P/E ratio number is read as "times", e.g., 10 times or 20 times earnings. This means investors are willing to pay 10 or 20 times a stock's EPS for a specific stock. The higher the EPS, the more expensive a stock is, and vice-versa.

If choosing between shares of stock of different blue-chip companies, the one with the lowest P/E ratio is the cheapest of them all. That stock would be the best one to buy at that moment.

Chapter 14

Corporate Valuation

One of the most important decisions business owners and management may have to make is selling the company or a unit of the company to other investors. And one of the most challenging decisions to make is determining how much to sell the company for, i.e., business valuation.

Why is business valuation such a tricky thing to do? It's because value is relative.

Take for example buying a second-hand car. The owner has a value in mind and the buyer has one, too, based on feedback from other people and sources like an online sales site or opinions of experts.

The best valuations are those that are as objective as possible and for this, numbers are crucial. Numbers don't lie so proposals with sensible numbers are often convey a high degree of objectivity when selling products and services. That's why the best valuations are those that are supported by sensible numbers.

Kinds of Valuations

There are three types of company valuations:

1. Discounted Cash Flows;

2. Market; and

3. Book Values

Discounted Cash Flow Valuation

This type of valuation is based upon a company or an assets future net cash flows or revenues. The basic principle is that given a reasonable market investment rate, investors will have to pay a certain amount of money now to receive specific sums of money or income in the future.

For example, if the current reasonable rate of return on investments is 10%, how much money does an investor need to pay for an asset that is expected to generate $100 thousand every year for the next 10 years?

Using the principle of discounting, you will get the present values of:

1. $100 thousand due after year 1;

2. $100 thousand due after year 2;

3. $100 thousand due after year 3;

4. $100 thousand due after year 4;

5. $100 thousand due after year 5;

6. $100 thousand due after year 6;

7. $100 thousand due after year 7;

8. $100 thousand due after year 8;

9. $100 thousand due after year 9; and

10. $100 thousand due after year 10.

These will give you:

End of Year	Expected Cash Inflow at End of Period	Discount Rate	Net Present Value
1	$ 20,000.00	5.00%	$ 19,047.62
2	$ 20,000.00	5.00%	$ 18,140.59
3	$ 20,000.00	5.00%	$ 17,276.75
4	$ 20,000.00	5.00%	$ 16,454.05
5	$ 20,000.00	5.00%	$ 15,670.52
6	$ 20,000.00	5.00%	$ 14,924.31
7	$ 20,000.00	5.00%	$ 14,213.63
8	$ 20,000.00	5.00%	$ 13,536.79
9	$ 20,000.00	5.00%	$ 12,892.18
10	$ 1,020,000.00	5.00%	$ 626,191.52
		Total	**$768,347.95**

The investor should pay $614,456.71 today to receive $100,000 annually at a discount rate of 10%.

This is also the same principle used to price bonds, US Treasuries, and other fixed-income instruments in the secondary market. For example, a US Treasury bond with:

1. A Face Value (Maturity Value) of $1,000,000.00;

2. A tenor of 5 years;

3. Coupon rate of 2%; and

4. Yield-to-Maturity of 5%.

With an annual coupon rate of 2%, the security will pay $20,000 annually to the owner of the Treasury bond for 10 years. At the end of the 10th year, the Treasury department will also pay the principal or face value of $1,000,000 back to the investor. Discounting these cash inflows:

End of Year	Annual Coupon Payments (+ Face Value at Maturity)	Discount Rate	Net Present Value
1	$ 20,000.00	5.00%	$ 19,047.62
2	$ 20,000.00	5.00%	$ 18,140.59
3	$ 20,000.00	5.00%	$ 17,276.75
4	$ 20,000.00	5.00%	$ 16,454.05
5	$ 20,000.00	5.00%	$ 15,670.52
6	$ 20,000.00	5.00%	$ 14,924.31
7	$ 20,000.00	5.00%	$ 14,213.63
8	$ 20,000.00	5.00%	$ 13,536.79
9	$ 20,000.00	5.00%	$ 12,892.18
10	$ 1,020,000.00	5.00%	$ 626,191.52
		Total	**$768,347.95**

Based on the discounted values of the cash flows at the end of each of the 10 year of the security's life, the price of the security at a yield-to-maturity of 5% is $768,347.95.

Now, let's apply this to an actual business. Let's say a restaurant is generating an average annual income of $500,000, which is expected to increase by 5% annually for the next 10 years. How much should an investor buy it for if the average annual returns on the stock market is 15%?

End of Year	Expected Annual Income	Discount Rate	Net Present Value
1	$ 500,000.00	15.00%	$ 434,782.61
2	$ 525,000.00	15.00%	$ 396,975.43
3	$ 551,250.00	15.00%	$ 362,455.82
4	$ 578,812.50	15.00%	$ 330,937.93
5	$ 607,753.13	15.00%	$ 302,160.71
6	$ 638,140.78	15.00%	$ 275,885.87
7	$ 670,047.82	15.00%	$ 251,895.79
8	$ 703,550.21	15.00%	$ 229,991.81
9	$ 738,727.72	15.00%	$ 209,992.52
10	$ 775,664.11	15.00%	$ 191,732.30
		Total	**$2,986,810.80**

The total of the discounted values each of the expected annual cash flows is equal to $2,986,801.80. If you want to buy this business, this is the ideal price to do so.

However, a business' income is neither guaranteed nor fixed and as such, you'll have to factor volatility into the pricing. Let's say that the standard deviation of its income is $50,000. If you want to be conservative about your valuation, the estimated annual net cash inflows or income would be:

End of Year	Expected Annual Income	Minimum Expected Annual Income (based on Standard Deviation)	Discount Rate	Net Present Value
1	$500,000.00	$450,000.00	15.00%	$ 391,304.35
2	$525,000.00	$475,000.00	15.00%	$ 359,168.24
3	$ 551,250.00	$501,250.00	15.00%	$ 329,580.01
4	$ 578,812.50	$528,812.50	15.00%	$ 302,350.26
5	$607,753.13	$557,753.13	15.00%	$ 277,301.88
6	$638,140.78	$ 588,140.78	15.00%	$ 254,269.49
7	$ 670,047.82	$ 620,047.82	15.00%	$ 233,098.94
8	$703,550.21	$ 653,550.21	15.00%	$ 213,646.72
9	$ 738,727.72	$ 688,727.72	15.00%	$ 195,779.40
10	775,664.11	$ 725,664.11	15.00%	$ 179,373.07
			Total	**$2,735,872.37**

If you want to be conservative about your valuation by incorporating the standard deviation into the projected annual income, the ideal purchase price for this restaurant goes down to $2,735,872.37.

Market Valuation

As the name suggests, market valuation refers to the value of the business in the market. The easiest and simplest way to value a business is by looking at the current price of its shares of stocks and multiply it by the total number of shares outstanding, i.e., market capitalization. If the current price of the shares of stock of Chumlee, Inc. is $50.00 and there are 1 million shares of Chumlee, Inc. that remain outstanding, then its market capitalization is $50 million, i.e., the market value of Chumlee, Inc.

The problem with market valuation is that it's subjective – really subjective. Why? A company's stock price is merely the general sentiment of investors of that share of stock and market sentiment isn't always objective. That's why they're called "sentiments".

Case in point, the recently favored company WeWork. By saying "recently favored", I mean that it's a company that was once the darling of the investing public, which quickly lost favor in the eyes of the investing public because of questionable practices and business models.

WeWork was valued by its biggest shareholder, SoftBank of Japan, at $47 billion at one point in time when its book value was way less than that. Why? Over optimism and to a large degree, investment bias. What business owner in his or her right frame of mind would value its business on the lower end of the spectrum?

Or how about the infamous "dot com" bubble during the 1990s? Many dot com companies were way overvalued by owners and analysts alike, hoping to cash in big time. This despite the fact that their balance sheets and income statements hardly contained assets of any great value to support such valuations.

Market valuation is only used for valuing real property investments and market-determined investments like publicly-listed stocks, bonds, and government securities. They're the most relevant form of valuation because at the end of the day, these assets will be sold to make money. Therefore, it only makes sense to assign a value based on how much they'd sell for in the market.

But how do you know an investment or a company is over, under, or properly priced? There are several ways to do so.

First is by comparing it with similar investments, businesses, or assets. For example, if someone's offering you an already operating Japanese restaurant in an upscale city for $500,000, you'll only know if the market valuation is cheap or expensive by comparing it a similar restaurant for sale, if you can find one. For a niche restaurant like this, it may not be that easy.

Or let's say you're choosing between shares of stocks of Apple and Samsung, two of the world's top consumer electronics manufacturing companies. By comparing them with stock prices of other consumer electronics companies in NASDAQ, you'll get a feel of whether they're overpriced or not.

When it comes to shares of stocks, however, you can't just compare stock prices. Why? You won't be comparing apples to apples and oranges to oranges. For example, the stock price of a company with big asset size will be higher compared to that with a small one. To properly compare them, you'll have to standardize them. You can use the Price-to-Earnings or P/E ratio for this.

The P/E ratio indicates how many times investors are currently willing to pay for the chance to earn a specific amount of dollars per share of stock (EPS). Hence, the P/E ratio is expressed as "times", e.g., P/E ratio of 4 times EPS.

The higher the P/E ratio, the more expensive a share of stock is and vice-versa. So, a company with a P/E ratio of 30 times is expensive compared to a company with shares that only have a P/E ratio of 20 times.

Why don't you try your hand at computing the P/E ratio by answering these?

1. If the current market price of a share of stock is $50 and its EPS is $5.00, what's the P/E ratio?

2. If the current market price of a share of stock is $70 and its EPS is $10.00, what's the P/E ratio?

3. If the current market price of a share of stock is $60 and its EPS is $15.00, what's the P/E ratio?

4. If the current market price of a share of stock is $10 and its EPS is $20.00, what's the P/E ratio?

5. If the current market price of a share of stock is $30 and its EPS is $30.00, what's the P/E ratio?

6. If the current market price of a share of stock is $20 and its EPS is $35.00, what's the P/E ratio?

7. If the current market price of a share of stock is $80 and its EPS is $40.00, what's the P/E ratio?

8. If the current market price of a share of stock is $90 and its EPS is $45.00, what's the P/E ratio?

9. If the current market price of a share of stock is $100 and its EPS is $50.00, what's the P/E ratio?

10. If the current market price of a share of stock is $40 and its EPS is $5.00, what's the P/E ratio?

When it comes to market valuation of fixed income securities or assets, the terminology is different. Instead of indicating the price or value in dollar terms, the convention is to price it by yield-to-maturity (YTM), which is expressed in interest rate form, e.g., 5%, 10%, 7.50%.

Another way that pricing fixed income securities is unique is that the higher the yield, the lower the value, and vice-versa. Why? YTM is used as the discount rate by which to determine the present values of all the future cash flows of such securities, i.e., coupon payments and face value. And based on the principle of discounting, the higher the discount rate, the lower the present value and vice-versa.

That's why the trading strategy for fixed income securities is buy high (i.e., at a high YTM) and sell low (i.e., at a low YTM). Effectively, this translates into buying at a low discounted value and selling at a higher discounted value.

Dis

Case in point, you buy a 10-year US Treasury Bond with a $100,000 face value, a coupon rate of 2%, at a YTM of 5%, the discounted value of which would be:

End of Year	Coupon Payments + Face Value at Maturity	Discount Rate	Net Present Value
1	$ 2,000.00	5.00%	$ 1,904.76
2	$ 2,000.00	5.00%	$ 1,814.06
3	$ 2,000.00	5.00%	$ 1,727.68
4	$ 2,000.00	5.00%	$ 1,645.40
5	$ 2,000.00	5.00%	$ 1,567.05
6	$ 2,000.00	5.00%	$ 1,492.43
7	$ 2,000.00	5.00%	$ 1,421.36
8	$ 2,000.00	5.00%	$ 1,353.68
9	$ 2,000.00	5.00%	$ 1,289.22
10	$ 102,000.00	5.00%	$ 62,619.15
		Total	**$ 76,834.80**

Your purchase price for this bond is $76,834.80. If you sell it at a lower YTM of 4%, the discounted value of all the remaining coupon payments plus the $100,000 face value would be: $83,778.21.

End of Year	Coupon Payments + Face Value at Maturity	Discount Rate	Net Present Value
1	$ 2,000.00	4.00%	$ 1,923.08
2	$ 2,000.00	4.00%	$ 1,849.11
3	$ 2,000.00	4.00%	$ 1,777.99
4	$ 2,000.00	4.00%	$ 1,709.61
5	$ 2,000.00	4.00%	$ 1,643.85
6	$ 2,000.00	4.00%	$ 1,580.63
7	$ 2,000.00	4.00%	$ 1,519.84
8	$ 2,000.00	4.00%	$ 1,461.38
9	$ 2,000.00	4.00%	$ 1,405.17
10	$ 102,000.00	4.00%	$ 68,907.55
		Total	**$ 83,778.21**

By buying at a YTM of 5% and selling it at a YTM of 4%, you would've made a $ 6,943.41.

Book Valuation

Book values are probably the most objective of all valuation models. It's because there's no hint of subjectivity as the numbers are all taken from the business' balance sheet accounts.

One of the most important valuations you'll need to do as a financial analyst is depreciable assets like building, equipment, improvements, etc. In a detailed balance sheet, you'll find an account called accumulated depreciation. By subtracting that from the purchase price of depreciable assets, you'll be able to get the depreciated or net book value of a company's fixed assets. And in most cases, companies depreciate assets across five years.

An entire company's net valuation is represented by its total shareholders' or stockholders' equity section of the balance sheet. This represents the remaining net value of the company's assets after paying off its outstanding financial obligations, i.e., debts. That's why companies whose liabilities exceed the value of their assets are considered bankrupt, i.e., their equity is already negative, which is worse than a zero balance.

For people who are buying into a non-listed company or are selling their shares of that company, book value per share is a good starting point because it's the most objective of all valuations. Total shareholders' equity is divided among the number of total outstanding number of shares to get the book value per share of a company.

Of course, the book value is hardly the final price at which non-listed companies or investors' shares of a company are sold. Buyers would like to get compensated for taking the risk of investing into the company by way of discounted prices while sellers often ask for a premium on their shares, especially if the company's already established and has a stellar reputation and financial track record already. It's the tug of war between the seller's and the buyer's interests that often set the prices at which non-listed company ownerships change. However, the book value provides the guide or benchmark for determining what a fair price is during negotiations.

The book value per share is computed by dividing total stock holder equity by total number of shares outstanding, while the company's net book value is its shareholder equity balance. Based on the financials of Vector Feeds, Inc. again:

Vector Feeds, Inc.

CONSOLIDATED BALANCE SHEETS

In Millions, Except for Fiscal Year-End Stock Prices

	2019	2018	2017	2016	2015
ASSETS:					
Current assets:					
Cash and cash equivalents	$ 139.55	$ 74.04	$ 57.97	$ 58.53	$ 60.34
Marketable securities	$ 147.75	$ 115.39	$ 153.98	$ 133.35	$ 58.52
Accounts receivable, net	$ 65.50	$ 66.25	$ 51.07	$ 45.01	$ 48.14
Inventories	$ 11.73	$ 11.30	$ 13.87	$ 6.09	$ 6.71
Average Inventory Levels	$ 11.52	$ 12.59	$ 9.98	$ 6.40	#VALUE!
Vendor non-trade receivables	$ 65.37	$ 73.74	$ 50.85	$ 38.70	$ 38.55
Other current assets	$ 35.29	$ 34.53	$ 39.82	$ 23.67	$ 43.10
Total current assets	***$ 465.20***	***$ 375.25***	***$ 367.56***	***$ 305.34***	***$ 255.37***
Non-current assets:					
Marketable securities	$ 300.97	$ 488.00	$ 556.33	$ 486.94	$ 468.76
Property, plant and equipment, net	$ 106.79	$ 118.01	$ 96.52	$ 77.17	$ 64.20
Other non-current assets	$ 94.22	$ 63.67	$ 51.93	$ 49.65	$ 41.23
Total non-current assets	*$ 501.99*	*$ 669.67*	*$ 704.78*	*$ 613.76*	*$ 574.19*
Total assets	**$ 967.19**	**$ 1,044.93**	**$ 1,072.34**	**$ 919.10**	**$ 829.56**
LIABILITIES AND SHAREHOLDERS' EQUITY:					
Current liabilities:					
Accounts payable	$ 132.10	$ 159.68	$ 126.41	$ 106.55	$ 101.40
Other current liabilities	$ 107.77	$ 93.39	$ 87.29	$ 62.93	$ 71.95
Deferred revenue	$ 15.78	$ 21.55	$ 21.57	$ 23.09	$ 25.54
Commercial paper	$ 17.09	$ 34.18	$ 34.22	$ 23.16	$ 24.28
Term debt	$ 29.31	$ 25.10	$ 18.56	$ 10.00	$ 7.14
Total current liabilities	**$ 302.05**	**$ 333.90**	**$ 288.04**	**$ 225.73**	**$ 230.31**

Non-current liabilities:

Deferred revenue	$ -	$ 7.99	$ 8.10	$ 8.37	$ 10.35
Term debt	$ 262.31	$ 267.81	$ 277.73	$ 215.51	$ 152.37
Other non-current liabilities	$ 144.29	$ 129.09	$ 115.47	$ 103.07	$ 95.51
Total non-current liabilities	*$ 406.60*	*$ 404.89*	*$ 401.31*	*$ 326.95*	*$ 258.23*
Total liabilities	**$ 708.65**	**$ 738.79**	**$ 689.35**	**$ 552.68**	**$ 488.54**

Shareholders' equity:

Common stock and additional paid-in capital, $0.00001 par value: 12,600,000 shares authorized; 4,754,986 and 5,126,201 shares issued and outstanding, respectively	$ 129.07	$ 114.86	$ 102.48	$ 89.29	$ 78.33
Retained earnings	$ 131.14	$ 201.14	$ 280.94	$ 275.33	$ 263.67
Accumulated other comprehensive income/(loss)	$ (1.67)	$ (9.87)	$ (0.43)	$ 1.81	$ (0.99)
Total shareholders' equity	*$ 258.54*	*$ 306.13*	*$ 382.99*	*$ 366.43*	*$ 341.01*
Total liabilities and shareholders' equity	**$ 967.19**	**$ 1,044.93**	**$ 1,072.34**	**$ 919.10**	**$ 829.56**
	$ 70.01	$ 79.80			
Net Working Capital	**$ 163.15**	**$ 41.35**	**$ 79.52**	**$ 79.61**	**$ 25.05**

Vector Feeds, Inc.
CONSOLIDATED STATEMENTS OF OPERATIONS
In millions, except number of shares which are reflected
in thousands and per share amounts)

	2019	2018	2017	2016	2015
Net sales:					
Total net sales	*$ 743*	*$ 759*	*$ 655*	*$ 616*	*$ 668*
*Theoretical Credit Sales	$ 314	$ 429	$ 371	$ 257	$ 343
Cost of sales:					
Total cost of sales	*$ 462*	*$ 468*	*$ 403*	*$ 375*	*$ 400*
Gross margin	$ 281	$ 291	$ 252	$ 241	$ 268
Operating expenses:					
Research and development	$ 46	$ 41	$ 33	$ 29	$ 23
Selling, general and administrative	$ 52	$ 48	$ 44	$ 41	$ 41
Total operating expenses	*$ 98*	*$ 88*	*$ 77*	*$ 69*	*$ 64*
Operating income	$ 183	$ 203	$ 175	$ 171	$ 204
Other income/(expense), net	$ 5	$ 6	$ 8	$ 4	$ 4
Income before provision for income taxes	$ 188	$ 208	$ 183	$ 175	$ 207
Provision for income taxes	$ 30	$ 38	$ 45	$ 45	$ 55
Net income	$ 158	$ 170	$ 138	$ 131	$ 153
Earnings per share:					
Basic	$ 0.34	$ 0.34	$ 0.26	$ 0.24	$ 0.27
Shares used in computing earnings per share:					
Basic	13,193.81	14,158.22	14,906.41	15,630.91	16,438.35

1. What is Vector Feeds, Inc.'s net company value?

2. What is the book-value-per-share of Vector Feeds' stocks?

Net company value for Vector Feeds as of end of fiscal year 2019 is $258.54 million. With total outstanding shares of 13.19 million, book-value-per-share is $19.60 dollars.

Conclusion

Thanks for buying this book. I hope that more than just reading about how to conduct simple corporate financial analysis, you actually worked on the case studies and exercises. That's because you'll only be able to truly understand and know how to conduct financial analysis through application and practice of what you learned. By working on the case studies and exercises I gave you, you would've had the benefit of both application and practice.

Corporate financial Mastering is both a science and an art. As a science, certain rules and procedures apply that result in the same results time and again. As an art, it involves interpretation of what the numbers indicate, which may vary from analyst to analyst, depending on their personalities, their knowledge of aggravating or mitigating factors, and to some extent, biases. But regardless if you think which characterizes corporate financial analysis more, the key is consistent practice. Though practice doesn't really make perfect, it can make you a corporate financial analyst expert in no time.

Again, many thanks and here's to your corporate financial analysis success!